TOTAL
PROSPERITY

TOTAL PROSPERITY

By
Rhett Smith

Rockhouse Press
New York, New York

ISBN: 1-59268-033-x

Rockhouse Press
New York, New York

An Imprint of GMA Publishing
GMAPublishing.com
Check out our website
A Global Publishing Company
Our books are available and distributed around the world and can be found on the internet at Amazon, Barnes and Noble and any major bookseller.

GMAPublishing@aol.com

Cover By: Cecilia Brendel
Manuscript Assistant: John Beanblossom

Printed in the United States of America

TABLE OF CONTENTS

INTRODUCTION

I WOULD FIRST LIKE TO start out by thanking you for choosing this book. It is your first step to reaching total prosperity. I can promise you this book will change your life and get you moving in a positive direction. The essence of this book is about how to get the most out of your everyday life for the short time you are here on this Earth. It has become apparent to me that the older we become the faster time seems to move. The sands of the hourglass seem to drain away without a fleeting glimpse of where the time went. When we were children the days and nights seem to never end and each day was a new adventure. Now the days and nights go by like single minutes on a clock and as another week passes by in your life we often wonder where it went or what we were able to accomplish. The answer we come up with is usually nowhere and nothing. I know this may seem a little depressing, but it is the plain truth and a reality for the massive bulk of people that we call Average. It is also the grim reality for those self-chosen less fortunate ones that we call under Average or under Achievers. The good news to this grim reality is that with every Yin, there is a Yang. By this I mean that every negative has a positive, and every positive has a negative. That is simply the law of the Universe. So the good news to this reality we live in is that with every week that passes by in your life at light speed in your routinely, boring, unfulfilled, and under-achieving life, there is always another brand new week just around the corner to make a commitment to yourself to change. By change, I mean to change everything. Change the way you manage your time. Change your frame of mind. Change your body. Change your business relationships and your personal relationships for the better. Change the way you eat. Change the way you manage you stress. Change the way you pray. Change your productivity. Change the moment in time you live in. When you begin to make these changes you will suddenly see your life around you begin to grow more prosperous. I would like for us to have a clear understanding of the true meaning of prosperous. The actual definition of prosperous is to thrive or succeed. I would like to twist the actual definition a little bit and define prosperous as thriving and succeeding, financially, spiritually, mentally, and physically. However, it is important to understand, you cannot have one and lack in the other. To be completely prosperous you must thrive to be equally mentally, physically, spiritually, and financially successful. I know we have all heard many examples of individuals being prosperous in one area but completely unsuccessful in another. The millionaire who is suicidal with misery; the successful politician who commits adultery; the beauty Queen that will always think something is wrong with her because see has no self-esteem; the family man who has a drug or alcohol addiction regardless of the loving wife and children that are waiting at home for him; the genius who has everything but self-worth; the star athlete who murders his wife; the famous actor who dies of a tragic drug overdose; the average 9 to 5 employee who lives out their entire life stuck in a miserable routine, only to grow old and wonder where all their dreams have vanished, never realizing they were only afraid to make a change. These are several grim examples of people that are prosperous in one area but are lacking significantly in another. The sour soul will eventually erupt like a raging volcano that devastates everyone who cares. These examples are your alternatives if you want to continue living each day lacking in total prosperity. I think I will choose E, none of the above. On the other hand you can decide to change and wring dry every bit of moisture that life has to offer. Living each day to it's fullest potential. Remember, you do not get a second chance, so act now. If I have your attention now I can tell you how we are going to make these changes.

It is important for you to understand the most important ingredient to making a committed change in your life is Action. You cannot simple read this book, get temporarily inspired and take no Action. This book is not going to do the changing for you.

This book is simply going to show you the door to change; you must be the one to walk through it. If you do not understand that you must take Action to reach total prosperity, then I would recommend that you do not read any further, because it will do you no good. For those fortunate ones that do understand what I am saying, let us continue down this adventurous road to change. To reach Total Prosperity in your life, you need to commit yourself to mastering these ten life-changing categories. *TIME MANAGEMENT*, this skill alone can make vast changes in your life if mastered correctly. Your *RELATIONSHIPS*, business and personal, are they fulfilling and happy? *SPIRITUAL HEALTH*, do you enjoy and respect the beautiful things nature has to offer you? Do you ever take time to watch a beautiful sunset? Do you have strong faith in your beliefs? *PHYSICAL HEALTH*, do you exercise your body often and correctly? *STRESS MANAGEMENT*, are you managing your daily stress properly? Your overall *FRAME OF MIND*, how often do your thoughts remain positive throughout the day? *LIVING IN THE MOMENT*, do you live your days out in the present moment or do you constantly regret on the past and worry about the future? *DIET*, what we put in our body will be our daily energy source, are you eating properly and healthy? *CREATIVITY*, is your imagination still active? Do you stay creative throughout the day seeking opportunity and ways to better your life? *PRODUCTIVITY*, are your daily actions productive on and off the job? Well there it is, ten simple solutions to reaching your personal total prosperity. We have all heard of these solutions numerous times and are probably familiar with some, if not all of them. So why if it is this simple and straight forward is everyone not getting the most out of everyday life? That is a good question, and I believe it is because we do not take proper Action on making these solutions a part of our everyday life.

To combat this no action syndrome, I have included a simple solution. It is called a daily report card and it is attached at the back of this book. I chose a report card because it is a straightforward and honest way to see your action in progress. Do you remember the kids who made straight A's in school?

Do you remember the dedication and sacrifices they made? That is the kind Action and dedication I want to see out of you. The only stipulation is that I do not want you to use this report card until you have read the chapters on each subject. I want you to have full understanding of each subject and what it means to live without each particular category and what it means to live with each category. When this book is completely read, you can then begin to use the daily report card. At the end of the day grade each category on the report card, and remember by cheating, you are only cheating yourself. I encourage you to grade very strictly. At the end of each day your grade will become cohesive to how your day unfolded. I can personally guarantee that if you begin to have a consistent A at the end of each day in your life, you will begin to see a dramatic change around you and within you. You will then start approaching ever so close to total prosperity. Do not worry, and believe me, you will know when you get there. Remember, it is not so much as where you end up, but the direction you are headed in. If you are in the right direction it is inevitable that great things will start to happen. Keep in mind that this is not a school grade on how well you were able to memorize something said or something read this is a grade on your life! Good Luck and enjoy the changing process.

Chapter 1

TIME MANAGEMENT

TIME MANAGEMENT IS ONE OF the key components in reaching total prosperity. Mastering this skill alone can begin to make drastic improvements in your life. For the sake of this chapter, let us define Time Management as *accomplishing the maximum of your daily task, day-by-day, hour-by-hour, and minute-by-minute, by focusing on your results more than your actions.* You see, a person can try to feel busy all day, but in reality, they never really have a plan of task accomplishment, they just appear to be working strenuously. These people more or less focus on actions, just trying to keep themselves busy. They never truly have an idea of the tasks that actually need to be accomplished. At the end of the day, they are completely tired and thinking, "there is so much more to be done and so little time to do it, I guess I will get to it tomorrow." This is the time crisis reality for the majority of people in this world, but it does not have to be that way. With a little self- discipline and knowledge, you can begin to beat the clock and take control of your time and your life. Proper Time Management can allow you to become less busy and accomplish more, to be more in control of your life, to gain respect from your employers and colleagues, to have plenty of leisure time, to find and accomplish your dreams. Time Management skills can be broken down into three P's, one to avoid, and two to embrace. They include: procrastination, planning, and priorities. Procrastination is the negative P you must avoid and ultimately remove from your life. Planning involves mapping out tasks you want and need done. Understanding your Priorities is an awareness of your most important tasks to your least important tasks. When you can learn to eliminate procrastination from your life and fully understand the Time Management skills, planning and priorities, you will become a true Time Management artist. Your life will become more focused, clear, and organized. As a positive reaction to this, your prosperity will increase and your daily stress will decrease. Bringing your life closer to Total Prosperity.

PROCRASTINATION

The three P's of time management include two positive skills and one very negative skill. The negative P of Time Management is a familiar word in our society called *procrastination*. I believe in getting the bad news out of the way first, so the last thing in your mind to think about will be the good news. Procrastination is what makes the large number of average people so large. For if no one had the habit of procrastination, there would be great accomplishments in our society daily, by any given individual. Everyone would be an overachiever. Unfortunately, this is not the case. What usually happens is the great masses wake up, have a pretty decent idea of what needs to be done, put it off until a later date, come home, watch TV, and go to sleep. Scary huh? Throughout your journey to reach Total Prosperity, procrastination can be one of your biggest enemies. There must be a great deal of importance put on this treacherous habit. Procrastination will be one of your Red Alert enemies so to speak. From this sentence forward in your journey, you need to train your brain to detect the slightest amount of procrastination. When procrastination comes up, a Red Alert signal needs to go off inside of you saying, " STOP procrastinating, do it now and it will be done, do it now and you will begin achieving". Remember procrastination is a habit, on the opposite end, achieving is a habit. It is very possible to eliminate bad habits and create positive habits in your life. Procrastination is nothing more than a bad habit. That is reality! Procrastination must be defeated, and vanish from your life completely. Do not worry; I am not going to let you try to defeat this habit of procrastination blindly. I will explain to you the true nature and origin of procrastination. If you understand where something comes from, and why, it becomes much easier to destroy. Procrastination gains its strength in many places. Procrastination resides in your fears, indecisions, difficulties, and lack of focus. It will be much easier to eliminate this awful habit from your life once you completely understand why procrastination gains power in these areas.

Procrastination resides in your fears. It gains power from your fears of happiness, of failure, of recognition, of change, and the unknown. People cannot face the consequences of what it may mean in their lives if certain things are accomplished. They become comfortable in there life, and resist any change, even if they are unhappy. A bit perplexing isn't it? A person that is unhappy but refuses to change out of mere comfort and convenience. They are so completely addicted to procrastination that they welcome it into there home, looking for a new excuse to put anything they can off, for that moment to sit on the couch and ponder how bad their life is.

People put off accomplishing things in their business career out of a fear of success. They want to get their resume' up to date and search for new careers with new companies, but they continually tell themselves they are too busy to do it right now. The truth is, deep inside they are deathly afraid of what might happen if they actually get that better paying. *What if I do not like it? What if my new piers do not like me? Will I have to move? What will my life be like if I make that kind of money? Will I be able to handle it? What if I miss my old job and cannot come back?* These are probably a few fearful questions that might be running through their head. Next thing you now they are completely paralyzed in fear, a few hours pass, they look at the clock and say, "ooh, it's getting late, I need to go to bed". Absolutely nothing got accomplished. This sequence is repeated several times a week, perhaps nightly, until this poor soul is ready for their steady pension from their same unhappy job, all because their fears of success welcomed procrastination into their lives.

3

Another common fear is a fear of failure. People become so afraid of how they will feel if they fail at a particular achievement that they consider it not worth trying, or simple putting off. They begin to think, *What if it is too hard? Will people call me a loser if I cannot do it? Can I mentally handle failing? Do I have a good excuse if I fail?* Next thing you know their fear has focused their mind so hard on failing that the achievement of consideration is swept out of their minds and constantly put off whenever thought about again.

Many people fear the unknown. They fear the unknown of what is around the corner, and they fear the unknown of what is inside of them. For example, through your journey to destroy procrastination, your fears of the unknown may begin to ask, *what will my life be like if I never procrastinate again? Will I like that new life? Is it going to be too hard? Do I really have what it takes? Can I really change and become more successful? What does an over achiever think and feel like? Will I like being an over achiever? Can I handle all of this?* Next thing you know all that fearful thinking as brought on another case of paralysis by fear, resulting hopeless procrastination. Nothing is done, and you go to bed worrying about all the things that need to be done in your life.

This leads to a never-ending cycle, you become like a dog chasing its tail profusely, alone to wind up exhausted, physically and mentally, in the exact spot you started in. These fears are severely detrimental to your overall happiness and accomplishment in life. Procrastination nurtures strength from these fears until your submission. Once we destroy these fears, procrastination will become a considerably weaker force to battle. There are techniques that can help you defeat these fears. When the next achievement comes up in your life, be it big or small, listen to what the voice inside you is saying. If it is throwing fearful thoughts back and irrational reasons for you to procrastinate, argue those reasons. Argue those reasons with a passion, even if you do not agree. An example: After a heavy dinner with your significant other, you suddenly realize you have let yourself become significantly overweight. You go to bed somewhat depressed about your metamorphosis into the up and coming Sea World attraction. When you wake the next morning, you are determined to lose 25 to 50 to 100 pounds over the next several months. You tell yourself I am going to do it, but somewhere deep down your subconscious is saying, "no way, it cannot happen, you are too out of shape, you haven't got the time, you don't want to change your eating habits, this will be way to hard." Before an argument can even begin, your outer conscious, the conscious you know as you, is agreeing, "yea, your right, I don't want to change my eating habits, this is going to be to hard, I have better things to do with my busy time." Next thing you know the notion of achievement is over, and you go back to your demoralizing, comfortable routine. A better alternative: When this subconscious voice, which only you can hear, begins to say these things, you argue the point, whether you agree or disagree, *"no way, it cannot happen."* "No, where there is a will there is a way, it can happen, it will happen." *"You are too out of shape."* "I am not that out of shape and I know I can get in better shape." "You haven't got the time." "I will make the time!" *"You don't want to change your eating habits."* "I may not want to change my eating habits, but for the sake of my health, I have to change my eating habits." *"This is going to be too hard."* "Anything worth doing in life is never accomplished with ease." That is the way the argument should go. Even when you agree with your subconscious, you should still try to counter argue its fearful and paralyzing points. The subconscious is not used to being confronted and interrogated. When this happens the subconscious fear system begins to malfunction and weaken. You will begin to find that the subconscious questions begin to change and become less fearful and more positively focused. Have patience, this will not come overnight, and your subconscious has controlled these internal conversations for a long time. After a few rebukes with the fearful questioning you will begin to see the subconscious agree with an increasingly positive counter response. When this begins to take effect, you will have destroyed procrastinations major lifeline, *Fear*.

Fear is procrastinations primary energy source. There is only one problem; procrastination has more than one energy source. Procrastination can gain strength from indecision. People will simple procrastinate because they cannot make up their mind. For example: You need to paint your guest room. "What color should I paint it? Red, yellow, blue, green, there is so many to choose from? I never knew making a decision could be this difficult. I guess this project is going to take a few months. Since I have a few months, I will figure it all out tomorrow, and so the story goes. Once again, you find yourself chasing your tail, winding up exactly where you started. Due to indecision, you become paralyzed from accomplishing your task. You see, even though indecision is a different energy source for procrastination, they all have the same ending result, paralysis. To break out of indecision, you should force yourself to make a concrete decision on the task of accomplishment and stick with it. If it is painting your guest room, do not let yourself leave the store until a decision has been made. Do not second-guess yourself once the decision is made. Decide on it and then do it.

Procrastination gains energy from difficult, unpleasant and complicated task. You know you need to clean your house, file your taxes, balance your finances, make a budget, mow the lawn, study, etc... The thoughts of actually doing these things can become very grim. These grim thoughts can lead to total paralysis of the particular task. The irony is, the main portion of the unpleasantness is all created in your mind, not the actual reality of doing the task. The fact of the matter is these unpleasant tasks are rarely as unpleasant when you are in the actual process of accomplishing them. The reward you receive from within when the task is accomplished is far better than the weighted feeling of guilt and gloom you experience with a task left unaccomplished. You can defeat this procrastination response in several ways. First, when it is time to accomplish the task, tell yourself, "it is not going to be as bad as I am making it." Create games for yourself while you are doing the task, make it as fun as possible. You will be surprised how fun you can make any task if you really focus on enjoying yourself in the process. Give yourself a reward, to create a positive reinforcement, for a job well done. If a task becomes too overwhelming, you can break the project up into small stages. This will make the task much easier to accomplish. Accomplish one piece of the puzzle at a time until the large task is completed. Remember, the majority of the difficulty in a task is all made up in your mind.

Lack of any focus or interest, are two more areas procrastination loves to gain strength. Either you have no interest or focus in accomplishing the task or you simply forget to do the task until it is too late. Even if the task is uninteresting to you, there should always be the questions, what will it mean in my life if I accomplish this? How will I feel after this task is accomplished successfully? These questions should have positive answers to them. For example, you have thought of finishing school, but really have no interest or focus on accomplishing this task. You then ask yourself these questions. *"What will it mean in my life if I accomplish this?"* The answer will probably be, "a better career path making more money, meeting new people, learning new things, and a new life, with new challenges." *" How will I feel after this task is accomplished successfully?"* " I will have a new feeling of high self-efficacy, and more confidence to take on life's challenges." When you begin to realize the reality and the rewards of your answers to these questions, your mind will begin to gain focus and interest on the accomplishment at hand. You can then go after the accomplishment without any unwanted paralysis caused by lack of focus and interest. Where there is no paralysis, there is no procrastination.

As you can see, procrastination can take many forms. Every form of procrastination leaves you with nothing being accomplished and a feeling of low self- efficacy. Remember that procrastination is a habit. Habits can be broken, but only if new ones are there to take its place. Now that you know where procrastination gains power, it will be much easier to eliminate from your life. From here on, make a conscious effort to implement these procrastination-destroying techniques in your daily life.

PLANNING

Planning is the first positive P to learn in order to master proper Time Management skills. Remember, just as Procrastination is habit forming, so is planning. Planning will be your method to accomplishing your designated task. It will be your personal designed route to accomplishment. The majority of people have great ideas in their minds of task they want accomplished and task they need accomplished. Ideas of things they would like to do, places they would like to see, and people they would like to meet. The problem is, all these great ideas of accomplishment and adventure will very rarely happen. The reason being is improper planning or no plan at all. Maybe these people are unaware of the importance planning and time management. Maybe these people are just lazy and do not want to plan. Maybe these people just enjoy crisis in their life. For whatever the reason, techniques exist that can help you overcome it and understand proper planning skills. Techniques that will help you overcome improper planning skills or no planning skills at all, include: Being concrete and definitive in your ideas and speech, creating more time, problem planning, properly delegating task, and making daily to-do-list. Having a strong understanding of these techniques will increase your understanding of time management, and it will allow proper planning to become a part of your everyday life.

Becoming concrete and definitive in your ideas and speech is a major factor in proper planning skills. Let me give you an example: A young man and his wife would like to accomplish the task of taking a trip to Disney World. Over a dinner conversation, they talk with one another of how fun it would be if they could go on vacation there someday. They never talk of certainties or actualities; they more or less speak in fantasy mode as if it would never actually be a reality. The husband probably says, *"Yes, that would be a great trip to Disney World honey."* The wife replies, *"Yes it would be lovely, maybe this summer or something we can look into it?"* Husband replies, *"Yea, we will look into it this summer, maybe."* Meanwhile nothing much else is said about it. The summer rolls around and they mention as, *"we should have planned that trip to Disney World this summer like we talked about, oh well, maybe next year."* Next year rolls around and it is more than likely the same routine, the couple has a true desire to take a trip to Disney World, they do not plan properly or they do not plan at all, and they never go. For the trip to become a true reality, the conversation should probably go something like this. Husband replies, *"yes, that would be a great trip to Disney World Honey."* The wife replies, *"yes it would be lovely, let's do it this summer. How does the 15th of June sound? I will do some research next week to find the best place to stay."* Husband replies, *"I will put in for the time off at the office in the morning and start checking the best places to visit while we are down there."* Meanwhile, the summer rolls around, they have booked reservations on the 15th of June, the bags are packed and they are on their way, all because of proper planning. If you noticed, the second conversation contained no maybes. It was concrete and definitive. The maybes in your mind, about accomplishing task, are the killer. When a maybe is present, it changes everything. Maybes give you an excuse to never make an actual plan to accomplish the task or to just put it off. When you are concrete and definitive in your speech and ideas of task accomplishment, proper planning begins to occur. When you begin to form a plan for your task, you become closer to the accomplishment becoming a reality. Just as the wife found the best place to stay in Disney World and booked reservations. Then, when the couple talks about going, it is much more a reality with actual reservations. They really start to believe they are going, and the planning process becomes more in depth, bringing them closer and closer to the actual accomplishment. Being concrete and definitive will make proper planning become almost automatic in your life.

One way to quickly improve your time management skills is to simply create more time throughout the day. Now the concept of this is easy and simple, but it will take a good deal of self-discipline on your behalf. The most effective way to create more time is to wake up earlier in the morning or stay up later in the evening. To master time management skills successfully, a person needs to have a minimum of a sixteen hour functioning day. An example would be, 6 o'clock a.m. to 10 o'clock p.m., or 7:30 a.m. to 11:30 p.m. A functioning day can be defined as the time you are awake and ready to perform a task. Functioning begins when you are awake and out of the bed. When you are awake and in the shower, even if you still feel asleep, you are functioning. The day has begun. Therefore, lying in the bed wrestling with the snooze button or listening to the radio, even though you are awake, does not constitute the beginning of the day, because you have not begun the functioning of a task. To begin, simply check your normal schedule. If you already get up early, then check the time you are going to sleep. Make sure you are getting a minimum of sixteen hours of functioning. This may be a little difficult at first, but I promise you it will get easier once your body adjust to the change. So be patient with yourself and realize at first, you may be bit more tired at the beginning and end of the day. As time goes on, the body's energy levels will adjust to your new schedule. Once your body has adjusted to this new schedule, you can begin the more advanced time creator. This is simply trying to maintain an eighteen to nineteen-hour functioning day. An example would be, 6 o'clock a.m. to 12 o'clock a.m., or 7 o'clock a.m. to 1 o'clock a.m. This may seem a bit impossible, but with a little practice, it can be done. A recommend the more advanced time creator only for individuals who desperately need more time to accomplish a particular task, or for the individual who has maintained a sixteen-hour day for quite some time and still feels their time management needs are not being met. By creating more time, you have simply created more time for task accomplishing, and the more time for task accomplishing, the more task that get accomplished. If you are skeptical about this and you think it is not going to make a difference, I can assure you it will. Just realize if you get up a half an hour early everyday for a year, you have created seven and half days of extra time. That is over a week of spare time that did not previously exist. It will make a difference!

To become an expert planner, you will need to do more than just planning for task that need accomplished throughout the day. You will need to acquire the ability to effectively plan for problems that may arise throughout the day. Becoming an effective problem planner will allow you to leave nothing in the day to chance. I am sure you are already aware that most days to not go quite as smoothly as planned. It can look so good on paper, but when the day gets going, it becomes a bit more difficult than you had originally planned. I attribute the majority of this unexpected daily difficulty to events that you were unable to predict, unexpected events that seem to take up a considerable amount, if not all, of your time that you factored for your daily task accomplishments. Unexpected events such as interruptions, sickness, accidents, distractions, emergencies, sudden more prioritized task, cancellations, and breakdowns of anything vital to your time. The first way to overcome these unexpected difficulties is to realize that they do exist, and they exist daily. By going into each day with an awareness of unexpected difficulties, you will automatically have a mental advantage when they occur. The next step is to try to factor these unexpected events into your daily time schedule as accurate as possible. It is virtually impossible to factor in unpredictable events to 100 percent accuracy. If this were not the case, they would not be called unpredictable events. However, you can factor in unpredictable events to a point where they do not effect the day quite as significantly as they would have if they had not been factored in. There are many simple techniques to aid you in factoring in problems throughout the day. You already know the most important technique is to be mentally prepared for problems before they occur. Other techniques include, factoring problems into your daily routine, giving yourself proper time between task, leaving task accomplishment time free of interruptions and distractions, setting guidelines and rewards for task accomplishment, and avoidance of unnecessary problems by tailoring your specific task area for optimal results.

If possible, never put task back to back on your time schedule. Say you have planned an hour meeting starting at nine o'clock a.m., and another meeting thirty minutes away starting at 10:30 a.m., this leaves you virtually no time for error to make your 10:30 appointment. The slightest thing can go wrong and the day suddenly turns into a confused and hurried mess. I am aware that sometimes this tight scheduling is simply unavoidable, but I recommend that you only use such a tight scheduling pattern in must situations.

Another good technique is to try to leave time factored for task accomplishing free of distractions and interruptions. If you have to study or finish a critical project at work, do not turn the radio or television on, try to leave your phone off if possible, and pre-warn friends, employers, co-workers, and other potential interrupters that you will be extremely busy during this particular time. This will allow you to put up a do not disturb sign so to speak. If interruptions become unavoidable, try to ask the interrupter if it is possible, you can get back with them as soon as you get the particular task accomplished.

If you begin to feel distracted, try to set guidelines and rewards for yourself until the task is completed. You can tell yourself no television, web, hobbies, or socializing until the task is completed, and you can give yourself rewards for completing the task. I remember during my college years, I would virtually go missing from everyone while studying for an exam. During the completion of the exam, if I felt I had prepared myself thoroughly, I would always treat myself to a nice steak dinner as a reward. I used this reward as a mental incentive for myself to maintain focus and avoid distractions during difficult studying sessions. To this day, I still implement this reward for a job well done.

A simple technique that will help you avoid problems before they start is to tailor your specific task area for optimal results. If you know you will be studying for a big exam, plan to take it to the library, or a place you find you can best concentrate, do not plan to study at the frat house and expect it be effective, smooth, and problem free. If you have a lunch or dinner appointment with a customer you are familiar with, tailor it to their particular personality. If the customer is older and easily disrupted, go to a place that is quiet and non-congested. If the customer likes to eat, and is more attentive when the food is plentiful, go to a buffet or place of large meals. If the customer is young and vibrant, go to a place that has a friendly party atmosphere. I think you get the picture, by tailoring the particular task area to yield optimal results; you can avoid many unnecessary problems.

Remember, to become an excellent planner, you need to learn the art of problem forecasting. The art of problem forecasting involves knowing when to implement these techniques. If you can go into each day prepared for problems, you will be one step ahead of the game before it gets started. Implementing these problem-planning techniques will allow your planning skills to flourish.

There are certain days and weeks in your life when it is virtually impossible for you to accomplish everything that needs to be done. When this happens, it is time to implement the planning skill of delegation. Delegation involves transferring responsibility of task accomplishment to others. I highly recommend this technique when the daily and weekly load is just too much; when you need a second opinion; when you have someone more competent to complete the task; and when you want a little extra time for yourself. When forming your daily schedule, decide what task you feel are able of delegation. Delegate the jobs you feel are of less importance, and will take too much of your time. If you are in a position of managing complex jobs, delegate them to the employee with the greatest skill in that particular department. When you become a good delegation planner, you will find more and more time available for accomplishing task that are of most importance to you. To delegate properly, you will need to explain the task in detail. Exactly what needs to be done, and when it needs to be done. The only time it will be necessary to reprimand the individual involved in the delegated responsibility is when you know that you explained the job and the timeline thoroughly and the individual acted negligently. Once you have delegated and explained the task thoroughly it is time to let go, stop worrying, and trust the individual is capable of completing the specified task. The actual definition of delegate is, *entrust to another*. Therefore, you should do just that, entrust it to the delegated individual. Always reward the individual for a job well done. Be it verbally or materialistically, never let good jobs go unnoticed. This rewarding, will give the individual extra incentive to do a good job for you in the future. Without any type of rewarding process, the individual will begin to wonder why they are working so hard for someone who never notices. Proper delegation is an excellent planning skill to acquire. When delegation is handled correctly, there will be more time to accomplish task of your importance, and a trust will accompany you that the task delegated will be completed efficiently and effectively.

Making daily to-do-list is another excellent technique in proper planning. Many people feel they can accomplish their entire daily task based off memory alone. This method simple cannot be repeated consistently with effectiveness. People simply get too busy or distracted day in and day out to remember everything that needs to be accomplished. It is pleasant first thing in the morning to have all these great ideas of the task you are going to accomplish for the day. It is not so pleasant when the end of the day arrives and you suddenly realize you have completely forgotten some of the most important task that needed accomplished. A great planner never leaves the house without a descriptive to-do-list. When you create your to-do-list, you should use calendars and daily planners.

Use calendars at home, work, and everywhere it is convenient. Study the calendars carefully at the beginning of each month. Try to get an overall outline of what you think your month will entail. Look for meetings, tests, bills, paydays, birthdays, anniversaries, parties, and holidays. This should give you an accurate idea of how busy each month will be for you throughout the year. At the beginning of a month that appears busy, you will know ahead of time that you need to be well organized and focused, and you can prepare for it accordingly.

Use daily planners to compliment your calendars. Just as a calendar creates a great monthly outline, a daily planner creates a great daily outline. The night before the beginning day, you should create your daily outline using a detailed daily planner. A good detailed daily planner will include the day and date, an hour-by-hour schedule, and plenty of room for notes and list in each days box. When you wake up in the morning, you should be able to look at your daily planner and have an accurate idea of what needs to be done, when it needs to be done, where you need to be, and when you need to be there. On those busy days, you can fully prepare yourself ahead of time to realize you will need to be extra organized and focused. This to-do-list should include everything of importance that needs to be done on that particular day. They can be in whatever order you want them, as long as they are written down and you realize they need to be done. However, I would recommend creating a daily to-do-list based on task of top priority to task of least priority. The most important task should be done first, and the least important task done last. I realize there will be times when it will be virtually impossible to accomplish task in that order, due to conflicting time constraints, but I still recommend listing your daily task from top priorities to least priority. If you cannot accomplish them in that order, at least you will be aware of which task are of most importance to you. Awareness of your priorities is as important as planning for them.

PRIORITIES

Understanding your priorities is a major factor in becoming a good manager of time. Priorities are the most important things that need accomplishing daily, weekly, monthly, and yearly. They are the tasks that take full precedence of your valuable time. Having a clear understand of what your personal priorities are will make you a stronger planner, and bring you closer to becoming an excellent time manager. Many people make a solid attempt to plan for events that need accomplishing, but they fail to categorize these events by priority. Merely planning for task that need accomplishing is not enough to become an excellent planner, it is imperative you are conscious of your priorities while you are planning. This will allow you to make better use of your time during your task accomplishing sessions. To become knowledgeable of your overall priorities, you must first understand your present place in life. Once you have gained an awareness of your place in life, you can begin to define your priorities for what you are living for, and what you should be living for. When you fully understand your place in life, and understand what you are living for, you can begin to set daily, weekly, monthly, and yearly time priorities for the tasks you need accomplished. The moment you become fully aware of your priorities, your planning process will become more concrete and effective.

The most important step in knowing your priorities is having a clear understanding of your present place in life. During our life cycle, we all go through many different stages or places. We go from babies; children; pre-teens; teenagers; young adults; adults; older adults; and senior citizens. During these particular periods of our life cycle, certain responsibilities come into our life at different times for each individual. We graduate high school, graduate college, find a career, get married, have children, take on a mortgage, and so on. When these occurrences begin to take place in your life, your priorities will shift to a new set of priorities and responsibilities. The key is to have awareness that these occurrences will cause you to have a new place in life, and re-adjust your priority schedule. Without this awareness of new priorities, you may find life more hectic and confusing. The sad truth is many people never come to this awareness. To better understand your place in life, you must ask yourself, *what is my stage in life right now?*

If you are a late teen about to graduate high school in the next year, it is time to put major priorities on your future. Ask questions such as, *do I want to go to college? Where do I want to go to college? What should I major in? What do I enjoy? What kind of career path should I take? If I do not go to college, where do I want to work? Will this job give me the advancement and recognition I need?* At this particular place in your life, the answer to these questions should be your major priority. You should become less and less involved with what everyone else is doing and if your piers will think it is cool if you do this or that. You should begin to take on an awareness that a major priority shift is taking place in your life, and the better you understand it and prepare for it, the easier the transition will be.

If you are unmarried, in your twenties, and beginning to look for a career, you should put priorities on questions such as, *what kind of money do I need to make to support myself? What job would I best enjoy? What are my passions? What is my best opportunity for knowledge and advancement? Where do I see myself at thirty?* Make these questions your main priority until you find the answers. As I have seen so many young people do times before, do not put your priorities on going out and continually searching for that perfect party, working a dead end job simply because it pays the partying bills. Do not have the mindset that you are in the early to mid-twenties and getting younger, it is simply not reality. The transfer from mid-twenty to full-adult stage seems to be one of the toughest transitions people will encounter. For some reason many people cannot put the good ole' high school and college days behind them, and they still hold their priorities and behavior in that perfect place in life. The tragedy is, it is not their place in life anymore and their priorities are far from being in order. The many who cannot make the transition will suddenly find themselves in their full-adult thirties, completely lost and left far behind from true success and total prosperity. To better make the transition I feel these people need to have the understanding that it is a new chapter in their life and yes, they may have to work a little harder, but this new chapter can be just as fun and rewarding as the chapters of your younger years.

If you are married, the priority should be on your husband or wife, you should ask questions such as, *how will this effect the both of us if I make this decision? How would I feel if he/she did what I am doing to me? Is this job supporting us to the fullest? What can I do to help him or her become more successful and happy in life?* This is a transition in life where your priorities and decisions affect two people, instead of one. Your priorities should be placed on you spouse and the best things for the both of you. Remember, you made the decision to get married, that means you made the decision to step up to the plate and take on the responsibilities and priorities that come along with being married.

If you are married and have children, the priorities shift to more than just your spouse. You should ask questions such as, *what does it take to be a good mother/father? How do I want my child to behave? What things to I want my child to see and learn? Is this job the best job for my family? What things can I do to make everyone in my family happy?* Here again, this transition will cause your priorities to shift on others, instead of just yourself.

If you are divorced and have kids, you should ask questions such as, *what could I do to give my child a positive understand of why we are divorced? How should I behave when I am around my child? What type of person should I look for, who will make a good secondary role model for my child? What things can I say and do that will make my child happy?* The priorities have shifted toward you and your child. By asking who will be a good role model? You not only include yourself, and the type of person you are looking for, but the type of person that will be a positive influence on you and your child.

Whatever your place in life, ask questions of yourself to get you thinking on the right track. By asking proper questions, you automatically get your brain thinking on the basis of task that are of most priority to task that are of least priority. Your planning process is most effective when you become aware of what tasks are of most priority and what tasks are of least priority.

The next step to understanding your priorities is to find out what you are truly living for. Again, this may change as your position in life changes, but the values behind them should remain consistent throughout your life. Write down all the priorities that have meaning to you, including: family life, moral values, spirituality, work, free time, love life, hobbies, and health. As you begin to look at all these priorities, start to analyze which is most important in your life to which is least important in your life, and be honest. In truth, you may find that your hobbies and free time take precedence over other more important things in your life. Once you have completed your personal and honest priority list, make a priority list of how you feel the order should look to live life in total prosperity. Rate them on a downward scale of from most importance to least importance. There may be quite a bit of variation between your honest priority list and the priority list you feel you should live by. Based on your honest priority list, try to accurately predict how much time each day, week, month, and year you have been putting on each priority. Then try to predict how much time you should be putting on each priority to live in total prosperity. I can give you a hint, the more priority you put on family life, spirituality, work, health, and moral values, the closer you will be to living in total prosperity. Remember, even though you rate a particular category high in your life, it may or should not be as high on your priority list as it presently is. For instance, if you have a wife and children at home, they should be your number one priority whether you want them to be or not. Your golf and poker game should not be your number one priority, leaving you coming home late every weekend night and night or two during the week. If this is the case, you must make needed adjustments to reach total prosperity. I am not telling you to give up everything you enjoy in life; I am simply telling you to possibly re-adjust your priority schedule. When you change your priority schedule, you will begin to devote the right amount of time to each. It is important to understand, what you are living for, is not necessarily what you should be living for. To reach total prosperity will require a sacrifice to change certain priorities in your life at the right times.

Now that you have an understanding of your place in life and what you are living for versus what you should be living for, you should begin to have a better awareness of your most important priorities. With a better awareness of your most important priorities, you can begin to put time priorities on each. Throughout your daily planning process, you can begin to prioritize each task. While planning, set daily time priorities for time you want to spend on things of most importance in your life. Set time priorities for things of least importance in your life. There will be priorities such as, projects to be completed at work that are simply unavoidable and will require a lot of your time. However, things like work projects, even if work is not rated highly on your priority list, should be highly prioritized, because it has spillover effects on things you do rate highly on your priorities. For example, if family life is number one on your priority list, it will be difficult to properly care for this priority without work. On busy workdays, you may have to transfer some of your leisure time to things of greater priority. The key is, try to allot time throughout the day for things of greatest priority in your life. When setting time priorities ask questions such as, *am I spending enough time on this priority? Am I spending too much time on this less important priority? Is there anywhere in the day I can transfer time to a more important priority? Will I be making the most effective amount of my time if I accomplish this priority now?* When your brain fully understands your inner priority list, you will automatically start to accomplish priorities in a more effective manner. When you begin to make up your daily to-do-lists, you will clearly be able to see what daily task needs the most time and attention and what daily task needs the least amount of time and attention. You can then set time priorities on each daily task. Tell yourself you would like to have a particular task accomplished in a particular amount of time. If it is a highly prioritized task, give yourself plenty of time to complete it. If it is a task of minimum priority, allow yourself a minimum amount of time to accomplish it. Do not put too much emphasis and time on task of least importance, and too less emphasis and time on task of greater importance. It simply makes no sense to put more time on least prioritized items than greater prioritized items. If you find a task of little priority is cutting into time allowed for a more prioritized task, drop it immediately if possible, and focus on the more prioritized task. Setting time priorities for particular task will allow you to get the maximum potential of your daily time. When you reach the maximum potential of your daily time, you will become an effective time manager.

CONCLUSION

Time Management is an ever-important component to reaching total prosperity. You must require a strong degree of self-discipline to follow the steps it takes to become an excellent time manager. There must be an absolute understanding and avoidance of procrastination. Excellent time management skills will require a profound knowledge of planning, and techniques that are involved in planning properly such as, having concrete and definitive ideas and speech; creating more time throughout the day; problem planning for unforeseen events; delegating task properly when possible; and making accurate daily to-do-list the previous evening. To have a better understanding of proper planning and superb time management skills, you must display an awareness of your priorities. Pinpointing your highest priorities and your lowest priorities will involve an understanding of your present place in life; what your are living for versus what you should be living; and setting time priorities for everything you do. Once you grasp an understanding of the three P's that are required to become an excellent time manager, you can begin to implement them in your daily life. A strong sense of self-discipline will become a necessity when you begin the implementation process. Remember, anything worth accomplishing in life does not come without some form of effort on your behalf. The implementation process may cause a drastic change in your life. However, if you can stick with the routine it will soon become a positive habit in your life. As time goes on, the process will become less and less difficult, which in turn will make superb time management skills second nature in your life. When you reach this point, you will find your days becoming more and more organized, you will get more accomplished, and you will create more time for the things that are of utmost importance in your life. Through your hard work and self-discipline to become an effective time manager, you will be taking a step forward in a positive direction. This positive step forward will allow you to become more confident in yourself and your abilities, bringing you one step closer to reaching total prosperity in your life.

Remember to always focus on the direction
you are headed in more than where
You are going to end up!!

Chapter 2

STRESS MANAGEMENT

LEARNING TO BECOME AN EXCELLENT time manager is your first step to reaching total prosperity. Learning to manage life's everyday stress is the second stage to reaching total prosperity in your life. Reaching total prosperity in your life is like putting together an elaborate puzzle, putting in one piece at a time until the entire picture is revealed. The closer you are to finishing the puzzle, the clearer the overall picture becomes. Each total prosperity category we discuss, shall be one piece of the total prosperity puzzle. The closer we are to the end, the clearer the path to reaching total prosperity will become. Stress management is another piece of the puzzle that will bring you closer to total prosperity. Learning time management skills aids in reducing daily stress. Reducing daily stress is merely not enough to reach total prosperity. To reach total prosperity, you must learn to completely control and manage your daily stress. Having a better understanding of stress will ease the difficulty of learning to control and manage stress in your life. *Webster's* defines stress in three ways: pressure or strain that tends to distort a body: relative prominence given to one thing among others: state of physical or mental tension or something inducing it. Stress can impair both the mental and the physical state of an individual's body. Sometimes stress will affect only the mental and emotional states or it will affect only the physical states, but the most common stressors will affect both the mental and physical states simultaneously. Physical stress can come in the form of illnesses, injury, impairment, toxins, and allergic reactions. Emotional or mental stress can come in the form of job changes, moving, separations, death or birth of family members, and any other significant change in your everyday life. The majority of these stressors have overlapping affects on the individual. For example, if you experience a severe physical stress by breaking your leg, it is more than likely that a form a mental stress will follow, such as depression. It is important to understand that these life stressors are impossible to avoid. There is no one on earth who is living a life completely free of stress. Daily stress will never be eliminated from your life, but it can be controlled. The first step to controlling your stress is to recognize that you are under stress. Many people live out there lives without every realizing they are under stress. They simply cannot put their finger on why they are feeling a certain discomfort in their life, and probably write it off as them being destined to feel bad the rest of their life or just the normal, tough part of growing older. Some people realize they are under stress, but cannot figure exactly what is causing or how to stop it. The stress continues as a fixed part of their everyday life. To stop this cycle, and learn to recognize stress, an individual needs to understand all the symptoms of stress. Once you learn to pinpoint the symptoms of stress, you can begin to focus on the causes of your stress. Stress can come in all different forms. By understanding the basic causes of stress, it will become much easier to pinpoint your personal stress. When you gain the ability to recognize stress in your life, and understand the causes of stress, you can begin to manage and control your daily stress. Controlling your daily stress can make your life much more serene. Stress management can do a number of other positive things as well; it can increase your energy levels; increase your longevity, give you peace of mind; fight off disease and depression; create better moods; incorporate daily calmness in your life; and help you sleep better at night. You will never reach total prosperity without the puzzle piece of stress management. When you have implemented stress management and time management in your life, the other pieces of the total prosperity puzzle will fall into place with the greatest of ease.

RECOGNIZING STRESS

The first step to understanding stress management is to acquire the ability of recognizing that you are actually under stress. When you are in tune with your body and realize the symptoms of stress, it is much easier to become an excellent stress manager. Stress can come upon us in many different forms. It is easy to get symptoms of stress confused with everyday emotions. Many times throughout the day, people may experience stress symptoms and never realize why or what is causing the uncomfortable feelings. The two types of stress are physical stress and emotional stress, these stressors general occur together but affect the body in different ways. It is imperative you understand the symptoms of both physical and emotional stress and begin implementation of proper stress management techniques. If these symptoms go overlooked or ignored the affects of long-term stress on the body can be serious threat to your health. Long-term stress can result in states of prolonged depression, fatigue, irritability, isolation, sullenness, and nervous breakdown. Your goal is to try to control the stressors before they reach the symptoms of long-term stress.

Physical stress is the first stressor to bring into conscious recognition. Many physical stress symptoms are nothing more than the changing of your body's chemical levels to get ready for a perceived action. A good example would be an adrenaline change in the body as it reacts to physical threat. Due to these chemical changes, many physical symptoms can become extremely unpleasant. These unpleasant symptoms include: rapid breathing and heartbeat; tense muscles; nausea and stomach tightness; cool skin, hands and feet; diarrhea; dry mouth; increased sweating; anxiety; nervousness, mild to moderate shaking. Although these symptoms can be unpleasant and unwelcome at times, they are nothing more than the body reacting to its primitive response of physical threats. You see, our ancestors had to hunt for food to survive. They had real life physical threats, everyday. There were times when either they were hunting ferocious wild animals or those ferocious wild animals were hunting them. These were times of great physical stress on the body. Adrenaline would pump rapidly throughout their bodies enabling them to react explosively, quickly, and precisely. This was an everyday occurrence for our unfortunate ancestors. Their bodies went through every physical symptom I listed above. Only those physical stress symptoms were used for pure survival. The problem that lies with this history lesson is that modern human beings still carry many of the same chemical responses as our former ancestors. In today's society, these chemical responses are actually irrational. The only time they are necessary is when your survival is at stake. Your co-worker getting your promotion is not a threat to your survival; neither is being stuck in traffic; someone breaking up with you; a tough exam; moving; or your mortgage, I think you get the picture here. When these irrational chemical responses take place, you have to gain awareness that they are nothing more than an irrational response to the particular situation, unless the situation poses as a physical life-threatening scenario.

Emotional stress is the silent stressor that can be a deadly killer if gone unnoticed. I like to refer to emotional stress as the silent stressor because it generally affects the mind before it affects the body. Emotional stress is less tangible than physical stress. There is a short-term over-the-counter remedy for just about every type of physical stress known to man. On the opposite end of the spectrum, emotional stress has very few remedies that are accessible to the common public and can be taken without any serious mental side affects. Emotional stress can come in the form of worrying and anxiety. These less-tangible mental stressors also include feelings of depression, suicide, weakness, low self-confidence, hostility, irritability, helplessness, and worthlessness. The problem is these are feelings of intense unease, but you cannot put your finger on one particular symptom. You just know you are feeling extremely uneasy. It is critical to realize any of these symptoms is a sure sign of an undermining stressor in your life. If these symptoms occur, they should not be put off as "you being weird" or "these anxiety attacks happen to everybody," they should be recognized, as a stressor in you life that requires attention. Before you learn to control these emotional reactions, you must thrive for a conscious awareness of all your emotional stressors. Once these emotional stressors enter into full conscious awareness it becomes much easier for your mind to find the true source of the problem to assure it is managed and controlled.

Physical stress and emotional stress can have a very detrimental affect on a person's life. If stress is left unrecognized, long-term affects of stress will begin to set in. Long-term stress on the body can result in states of prolonged depression, chronic fatigue, irritability and isolation, sullenness, and eventually nervous breakdown. If these symptoms are occurring in your life, it is probably due to some form of long-term stress. All of the symptoms of long-term stress can be cured with conscious recognition and acceptance of the symptom. It is important to admit that these symptoms are occurring in your life and realize the fact that you can control them. When you admit your feelings, it becomes much clearer to see what is causing these symptoms. Once you accept that you are experiencing these problems, it is much easier to realize what is causing them.

States of prolonged depression can make for a miserable existence on this earth. In a state of prolonged depression, life just does not seem to have any zest. No matter where you are or what you are doing, nothing seems to give you any enjoyment. Your daily failures are intensified and taken much more seriously. It becomes hard for you to find a reason to get out of bed in the morning, and a good nights rest becomes rare. Before you know it, all your thoughts are focused on the negative and your entire world is perceived as sad and hopeless. In this prolonged state of mind, you begin to think it is normal to think and feel this way. If any happiness sneaks into your world, you become quick to shut it out and feel as if it is abnormal for you to be happy. Prolonged depression can be reversed if it is consciously recognized in your life. This is a horrible condition, because during these spells it is sometimes hard to realize that this depression is not your true reality. The depression seems so real; you actually think the negative thoughts that go through your mind are valid. It is simply not the case; life is never as bad in reality as it is portrayed through negative thoughts. To overcome this depression caused by stressors, you must first admit to yourself that you are experiencing depression. Once you realize you have symptoms of depression, you mind will begin to key in on what stressor is causing these feelings.

A spin-off side affect of depression is chronic fatigue. This fatigue is not the same fatigue a person experiences when they get up early, work hard all day, and go to bed late. That is a feeling of positive exhaustion from exerting your body's potentials. Negative fatigue reacts in an entirely different manner. Negative fatigue or exhaustion can appear at anytime throughout the day and in many cases last all day. An individual who experiences this negative fatigue cannot get enough sleep to make it go away. They have a tendency to stay extremely tired and lethargic all day; at times having trouble keeping there eyes open. This fatigue makes it very difficult to get out of bed and function diligently throughout the day. People with fatigue symptoms can never gain enough energy and enthusiasm to last a day or even an afternoon. They have that feeling of just waking up in the morning all day long. During these spells of negative fatigue, it is normally not the physical body that is tired and exhausted, but the mind. When the mind is stressed out and depressed, it has a tendency to focus on negative thoughts all day. These negative thoughts eventually fatigue the mind, which in turn fatigues the physical body. When you realize this fatigue is not generally physical, but mental, you can start to focus on the stressors that are causing these fatigue thoughts.

Irritability and isolation are two more negative mood changes caused by long-term stressors. Irritability causes people to react to situations in a negative and irrational manner. You become easily annoyed with everyone and everything. A mild traffic jam or a discrepancy with a friend or loved one can result in major negative mood change where rage, anger, and frustration result. The meanness of these individuals can give off an extremely negative vibe; this negative vibe will bring everyone who encounters them down to a negative level, regardless of how good they are feeling before the encounter. These irritably reactions to people and situations will eventually push everyone around them away. Eventually pushing everyone away will result in feelings of total isolation. You begin to feel no one can possibly understand you, or what you are going through in life. The feeling that it is you against the world begins to set in and it takes you right back to a feeling of irritability against everyone and everything. These two feelings seem to work together and give each other energy. Irritability causes isolation and isolation causes more irritability. These feelings can be managed by understanding that irritability is nothing more than overreacting to individuals and situations, in turn, this irrational overreacting causes a feeling of isolation, and stressors in your life are ultimately causing these feelings of irritability and isolation. When you realize that you do not have a chronic bad attitude, you only have a series of stressors causing this temporary mood change, it becomes easier to adjust and find the cause of the irritability and isolation.

Sullenness is another side affect of long-term stressors on the body and mind. Sullenness is a state of mind where an individual remains silent and dismal. Here again, this is another spin-off affect from depression or depressing thoughts caused by stressors. It would be quite difficult to have a sullen attitude if you were not depressed. The majority of the time these individuals are so caught up with negative thoughts about themselves and the world they live in that all their energy is focused inward, and strictly on the negative. When this occurs, the individual's personality and energy are stripped away leaving a gloomy presence for everyone to be around. Because of the negative energy around a sullen individual, people will eventually grow tired of being around these types of people. This in turn will create another cycle of isolation and irritation. If you find yourself growing less and less personable; your thoughts focusing on the negative; lacking any drive; and a more inward style of thinking where you are preoccupied with only thoughts about yourself and how bad you have it, then you are probably experiencing states of sullenness. When sullenness strikes, realize there is stressor behind this negative attitude change. You should then search and focus on what is causing this negative change instead of the negative thoughts that accompany this attitude. When your mind begins focusing on the cause, it can soon manage the stressor.

Possible the most severe symptom of long-term stressors is the eventual nervous breakdown. If stress continues unrecognized in your life, it will eventually lead to breakdown. Your body will go through all the symptoms of stress and eventually keep you in an anxious and depressed state until you finally breakdown physically and mentally. Breakdowns are not uncommon in high stress individuals, just as a well-made car will breakdown without regular checkups, so will your mind and body if stress symptoms are not recognized and managed. Nervous breakdown symptoms can include periods of manic depression, where depression is accompanied by periods of euphoria. The individual will appear very low and depressed and suddenly become very excited and overly aggressive. Periods of self-destructive behavior can take place during breakdown periods such as suicide, drug and alcohol abuse, spousal and child abuse, violent actions against people who care about you, ignoring or turning down positive opportunities, and feelings of losing control of yourself. If any of these symptoms become apparent in your life, even at small levels, you must realize you may have reached a point of being over-stressed. Focusing on your stressors can reverse this breakdown cycle. When you begin to focus on the stressors that are causing these symptoms of breakdown, you can then close in on every option you have to change these stressors, or manage these stressors to the point they do not affect your overall feeling of well being.

There are many different symptoms of stress. Behind every negative feeling involved in these symptoms is a stressor. In many cases, more than one stressor is causing these symptoms. Controlling and managing the stress is sometimes far less difficult than actually recognizing the stress. The hardest step involved in stress management is coming out of denial and making recognition with stress symptoms. When you can fully admit to yourself that you are experiencing stress associated difficulties on a physical and emotional level, you can begin searching for the cause. Once your personal stress symptoms are brought to full awareness, the cause will reveal itself with little difficulty. Understand this, your mind acts like a computer if rational thoughts are controlling it. When consciously say to yourself; "I am experiencing this negative feeling due to stressors in my life, not because something is physically or emotionally wrong with me." Then ask yourself, "I wonder what stressors in my life are causing me so much anguish?" "Am I afraid of something?" "Is there something I am doing in my life which I know I should not?" This questioning will set your mind on the path to seek out the stressors that are bothering you. In the process, the stress symptoms that you are experiencing will not have the same negative impact they would have on you if you were not consciously aware of why these feelings were taking place. When the stress recognition process is complete, you can begin to understand some of the basic causes stress. Understanding the basic causes and nature of stress will aid you in your search for your particular life stressors.

CAUSES OF STRESS

To fully understand the art of stress management, you must fully understand the causes of stress. Recognizing your stress symptoms is the first step to becoming a skillful stress manager. Once you recognize that you are experiencing stress in your life, it is time to begin the search for exactly what is causing this stress. Stressor can be caused by many different factors. Generally, there is more than one stressor in your life at any given time that is causing you problems. You may experience these stress problems either consciously or sub-consciously. A stressor consciously causing you problems is one that you are aware that something in your life is bothering you. Either you wake up everyday unhappy or you are feeling out of touch with yourself by constantly being pre-occupied with irrational thinking. Whatever the symptom, you are conscious of it. You may not know exactly what is causing these feelings, but you are aware that something is. Sub-conscious stressors causing you problems are more dangerous than the conscious stressor. In a conscious stressor, these individuals may not know that it is stress causing the problems but at least they have the awareness that something other than their life being miserable and without hope is causing the problem. Sub-conscious stressors give the individual a feeling of total helplessness. They are not aware that it is a manageable stressor in their life causing them problems; they merely think their stress related problems are irreversible, and their daily life becomes entirely negative and uncontrollable. Let me give you an example in the difference of conscious versus sub-conscious problems: Let us take two college students who are demanded to keep their grades at an optimal level. For the sake of this example, we can say the two are roommates. The two students attend the same classes and have the same demands of keeping their grades high. They also visit the same bars and parties on a weekly basis. Closing in on midterms they both begin to feel extreme stress symptoms. They are going through anxiety, bodily tension, and forms of depression. Student A is consciously aware that there are certain things in their life causing the uncomfortable feelings. Student A knows that he/she might be partying and drinking too much while trying to keep up the demands of excelling in school. Student A also knows that they are under pressure to do well on there demanding midterms. By consciously knowing this, student A begins to understand these symptoms better and they become less severe. Student A also starts to cut back on the partying and drinking to allow for better use of their time to study. In a short period student A's symptoms begin to dissipate and the demands of excelling on the midterms are met. During this time, student B is experiencing everything student A is. Only student B is not consciously aware that certain stressors are causing the uncomfortable feelings. Unaware that outside elements are causing these problems student B begins to grow more concerned of these uncomfortable feelings. The symptoms in turn grow worse and worse. Instead of cutting back on the drinking and partying student B begins to drink and go out more and more to try and forget about these stress symptoms. What student B does not understand is they are actually making the problems worse by trying to drown them out with drugs, alcohol, and late nights. Before they know it, they are completely unprepared for their midterms and the demands of excelling are not met. Student B begins to lose self-worth by thinking they are not keeping up with their demands, and the problems continue to persist and grow more intense. By understanding that something is causing these uncomfortable symptoms student A was able to yield an entirely different result than student B in the exact situation. Although student B was able to recognize symptoms of stress, he/she was unable to place these symptoms on particular causes. Some people have the ability to recognize their stress symptoms and immediately concluded the cause. Others can recognize symptoms or learn to recognize symptoms but never conclude the causes of these symptoms. Recognizing stress symptoms only makes the process of finding the causes of stress easier. For without recognition you can never understand that you are even under stress. As with student B, simply recognizing stress will not teach you to control stress, you must acquire the ability to both recognize stress and find the causes of stress. To acquire the ability of finding the causes of your stress, you must understand all the sources of stress. Stress may derive from many different sources, or you may have many different simultaneous stressors stemming form the same source. Sources of stress include: The most primitive form of stress, which is survival stress; internal related stress or mental stress; environmental stress or external stress; lifestyle related stress; and anger related stress. Understanding these sources of stress individually will allow you to better understand which source or sources are causing your stress. When you understand what is causing your personal stressors and can recognize the symptoms, you will then be able to learn stress management skills to control these irritable stressors.

Our oldest stressor is survivor stress. These stressors are our basic instincts to keep ourselves alive. When we are physically threatened, are bodies begin to adjust to the situation to give ourselves the best opportunity of survival. It becomes time for us to fight or flight. In a threatening situation, your body will begin to release adrenaline, which can cause feelings of extreme nervousness, diarrhea, and increased heartbeat. Adrenaline will also cause your body to mobilize sugars, which will temporarily give your body more strength and energy. This was a popular stressor in less civilized times. Survival stress was a daily experience, when human beings were hunters and protectors of their land. In modern times, the average person will very rarely experience this type of physical survival stress. They will generally confuse themselves to react very similarly to emotionally threatening situations. The fact that this stress response has been instilled in us from generation one, makes it difficult for us to realize our modern times very rarely require this type of response. When we are put under extreme emotional stress, our bodies become confused and perceive it as a life-threatening situation. The fact is this emotional stress is not life threatening at all. We just perceive the situation incorrectly. If someone is robbing you at gunpoint, it becomes a life-threatening situation. If you are laid off at work, it is not a life-threatening situation. These entirely different situations will however yield very similar bodily stressors to the average individual. Survival responses to physically and emotionally threatening events are one cause of stress, and later in this chapter, we will deal with overcoming this often-irrational response.

Mental stress or internal stress is a major cause of stress. This type of stress can come in the form of anxiety or daily pressures that cause your neurotransmitters to rise. Internal stressors can produce very uncomfortable feelings of helplessness and hopelessness. Your body and mind begin to fell very tense and uneasy, leaving it very difficult to function effectively throughout the day. This mental stress is brought on internally by the way you perceive situations. Here again, if you are experiencing a great deal of mental stress, it is likely your perceptions are irrational to the situations. These internal stressors can be brought on by many different personality characteristics. When you begin to feel the mental stress of daily pressures and your neurotransmitters increase, uncomfortable stress symptoms occur. This pressure can be brought on by feelings of perfectionism, fear of failure, and taking situations in life to seriously. Anxiety occurs when your daily life standards are not realistic, leaving your perceptions of situations irrational. Individuals who experience high amounts of mental stress generally believe they should be competent and in control of every situation; they believe every situation should turn out exactly as they had expected; they believe that things other than themselves cause all their unfortunate experiences; and they believe that their past failures will doom all future events. Mental stress and anxiety can cause great difficulty in peoples lives. With proper techniques, this type of stress is controllable, and when you learn to manage this stress, you will begin to perceive your life in a more tranquil setting.

Environmental stress is another common cause of stress. Environmental stress is caused by external factors. They are irritants in your daily living environment that can cause mental and physical stress related problems. Generally, these external stressors will cause physical stress, which will eventually lead to mental stress. In many cases, the individual is completely unaware that it is an external stressor causing them difficulty. These stressors can be caused by a number of factors. External stressors can come from household irritants such as allergens, uncleanly conditions, air pollution, and too much noise. They can come from job-related environments such as unhealthy working conditions, not enough personal working space, too much noise, and a stressful drive into the office. In unhealthy environments caused by external stressors, it is hard to maintain good productivity and stay positive. It is important to understand and analyze your external environment to seek out any unnecessary stressors that may exist. Once your external stressors are sought out, you can begin the process of managing them.

Lifestyle related stress is an externally related stressor. This stressor can come from your home or from your job. Many outside factors cause these stressors. Having more work than you can handle or less work than you are capable of causes them. Other causes include: career developments such as, job security, not enough opportunity or promotions, unclear job description, and over-promotions faster than you can prepare for; too many timelines or time constraints; your overall daily responsibilities; personal stress such as, financial problems and relationship problems; work related stress such as, too any demands from supervisors and customers, disruptions and distractions, and keeping pace with competitors and co-workers; lifestyle changes such as, births or deaths in the family, marriage or divorce, moving, job changes, children moving out, or health changes. If these lifestyle stressors continue unmanaged, fatigue and burnout will eventually occur. When burnout sets in, you will begin to lose interest in all daily tasks, leaving you with feelings of complete fatigue all throughout the day. Lifestyle stress can appear in many forms, it can take place at home and at work. More than likely, you are experiencing several lifestyle stressors daily. With time, you can learn to manage your personal lifestyle stress and bring your life closer to total prosperity.

Anger related stress is an internal and external related stressor. The stress is caused by external situations, but it is increased or intensified by your internal reaction to the situation. Daily anger occurs when frustrations begin to build up due to something or someone getting in the way of a desired goal or achievement. Anger or reacting angrily to situations can trigger anxiety; this anxiety can cause more anger and in turn create a vicious cycle. There are three basic types of anger, rage, resentment, and indignation. Rage is an uncontrollable and sometimes violent outburst of frustration. This rage anger may be expressed physically, verbally, or both. Resentment is a more subtle type of anger. This feeling generally occurs when one individual is jealous or resentful towards another individual or situation. These feelings are not expressed externally by verbal or physical expressions, but rather held secretively deep inside the individual. These feelings can cause a great deal of internal stress to the individual experiencing the resentment. Indignation is a more controlled type of anger. These are situations where you become extremely disappointed and the thought of expressing yourself irrationally is passed over for a more civilized response. Granite you are angry, but you let the feeling of rage work itself through your body and dissipate without causing alienation or discomfort to anyone. These types of anger can happen at any time, the important thing to understand is that how you react to the situation will result in the intensity of your anger. The calmer you react the less angry you will become, and the more intense you react the more anger that will ensue. Controlling and managing anger begins with the understanding that anger is not caused by external factors alone.

Understanding the causes of stress are as important as recognizing the symptoms of stress. Recognizing stress symptoms and understanding the basic causes of stress should work together in sequence. When you begin to recognize your personal stress symptoms, you can then begin to analyze what may be causing these symptoms. When you can learn to readily identify your symptoms and your causes, you can begin the process of controlling and managing your stress. To become an effective stress manager you must have a full understanding of your personal causes and the stress symptoms that are occurring due to these causes. It is much less difficult to manage and control something when you know what you are managing and controlling. If you do not understand what is causing your stress, it becomes very difficult to manage your stress. Stress management is more than just making naked attempts at managing daily stress blindly, hoping we get lucky and cure the unknown cause. Stress management is about taking the time to understand your life, becoming aware of every little detail that goes on in your life day in and day out. It is about being specific when searching for a cause, and completely understanding the symptoms that accompany this cause. When you begin to specify your stressors, there is nowhere for them to hide. Simply understanding the causes of your stressors will immediately decrease the negative affect they have in your life. When you begin to back these stressors in a corner, you can begin the process of managing and controlling stress everyday for the rest of your life.

MANAGING & CONTROLLING STRESS

Once you have learned the process of recognizing your stress symptoms and what is causing your stress, you can start the process of managing and controlling your daily stress properly. I think by now it is easy to understand that stress can come from many different angles. You may experience physical stress and emotional stress. More than likely, you are experiencing stress both physically and emotionally all throughout the day. The difficulty with stress is that we may not even understand what is causing it or why we are experiencing it. I hope that the first portion of this chapter has brought some light to you about what causes stress and what are the general symptoms of stress. If you do not think you are under stress, I would urge you to reevaluate your daily life and take a closer look, because it is probably not true. The mass majority of human beings experience some form of stress everyday, be it minimal stress, optimal stress, or too much stress. Our goal in this chapter is to teach you to thrive for optimal stress all day and properly manage stress when there is too little stress or too much stress in your life. By having a willingness to make positive changes in your life, mastering a few positive stress management skills, learning to control anger and frustration, and finding your optimal stress levels, you can meet your goal of this chapter and conquer stress once and for all. You will begin to see drastic positive changes in your life internally and externally when stress management is incorporated with time management. The overall puzzle of reaching total prosperity will begin to seem evermore clearer.

Managing stress will not come easy at first. Anything that makes improvements in your life never does. The reason it is difficult is that we are creatures of habit. We have a natural tendency to get set in our ways and resist any type of change. Conquering stress will require you to make a pact or promise with yourself to make a positive change. The reason I say it will be difficult at first is that you will have a tendency to try this for a week, regardless if you feel better or worse, and slip right back into your old ways again. For some reason or old ways and habits feel comfortable and require no effort. The problem is, your old ways and habits will get you absolulety nothing but the average misery in life. You will need to be patient with yourself and understand that if you happen to revert to your old ways of handling life, that it is just your habit and it will take some time and effort to break it. Through time, you will begin to develop new positive habits of handling your daily stress. When these new habits set in, you will find yourself wondering how you managed to get by so long maintaining your old habits of reacting to daily stressors. By having a willingness to change, you can keep yourself open for new opportunities and new ways of thinking. Keep the mindset of welcoming the changes you will experience when you begin to see the results of stress management in your life.

There are many stress management skills used to combat stressors in your life. By mastering stress management skills, it will be very difficult for stress to have such a negative impact on your life as it did before. Some key stress management skills include: forming a plan to manage your stress; creating a daily stress book; preparing yourself for daily stress; using mental imagery; learning to meditate; reducing the intensity of your reactions to stress.

The first positive stress management habit to form is to start making a daily plan to manage your stress. Sit down one night in a quiet place if possible and begin to evaluate your life. Make a list of the things that you want to change that are causing you stress. Having a written list of the things you want to change will allow your mind to begin to focus more intently on specifics. When we personally write down the things we want to change, we begin to feel a stronger commitment to amend these situations. This stress management plan is entirely personal and will vary from person to person. For example, if you are overweight and feel that it is causing you a great deal of stress, losing the weight you want to lose should be number one on your stress management plan. If your spouse is causing you stress, then your list should include sitting down with him/her and communicating any problems there may be. You cannot properly manage stress without a specifically written plan of the stressors you want to change in your life.

A daily stress book is another effective way to manage your stress. Each day that passes, carry a little booklet and write down events or thoughts that you found stressful. Write down how these events or pre-thoughts of the events affected you; what it did do to your state of mind; what it did do to your energy level; and how did you reacted to the event or pre-thoughts. During the course of this stress log, you may begin to see repeating patterns. Your reactions to situations and the way your reactions made you feel will begin to reveal the main stressors in your life. Your pre-thoughts of events ahead will begin to reveal the way you react internally. For example, if you have weekly meetings, your pre-thoughts before the meeting may cause unnecessary anxiety and energy loss, these thoughts in turn may cause you to not accomplish the things you wanted to accomplish in the meeting, causing more stress. If this pattern is repeating itself, you will want to highlight certain events and pre-thought reactions and consciously try to change these patterns. When you begin to consciously change these patterns you will begin to develop new and more positive ways to think and react to stressors. Without a daily stress book, you may never be able to pinpoint the stressors that are causing you the most problems. Your time and energy may be wasted on stressors that are actually not causing you problems at all. Once your stressors are brought under control, you will feel it unnecessary to constantly keep a daily log because you will be aware of how you are thinking and reacting to each of your stressors. At this time, you should know the most efficient way to think and react to the individual stressor.

Preparing for stress aids in effectively managing stress. If you walk out the door every morning planning for a beautiful stress free day you will probably be in for a let down. The fact is we experience a good deal of stress even on our best days. The most effective stress managers walk out the door everyday well prepared for the most difficult daily stressors and the stressors that sneak up unexpectedly. I am not telling you to walk out the door everyday to prepare for a miserable and awful day. I am simply telling you to be mentally prepared for stress that may arise. You can do this by simply planning for the stressors that constantly appear in your stress log and the stressors that you want to change in your stress plan. Go over these stressors in your head as a form of rehearsal; visualize how you want your thought patterns to be about the stressor and how you want to react to the stressor when it occurs. By being fully prepared for any daily stressor that may occur, you will be one step ahead of the stressor if or when it does occur. Your reaction to the stressor will be prompt and you will be effective at managing the stressor.

Imagery is another good technique to manage stress. Remember, are thoughts are alive. The thoughts that go through our minds cause physical and mental reactions in our bodies. Imagery can involve imagining yourself in a peaceful place during times of stress or times of unwinding. If severe stress begins to strike you can take a few minutes to take deep breaths and imagine sitting in a nice place such as a beach or a park. It may sound a bit silly at first but it really works. By you putting your mind in a peaceful place, your mind produces chemicals that are similar to the actual experience of being there. This results in a more relaxed state of mind. This type of imagery also works well in the unwinding process of a long day. You can put yourself in a dimly lighted place and begin to visualize peaceful things that will aid in your relaxation. Imagery can be used to properly imagine handling situations how you see fit. Great athletes will sit in a quiet area before a big game or match and imagine performing to one hundred percent of their ability. With attention to detail, they will imagine the feelings that are going through their bodies, the noise of the crowd, their opponent's reactions, and exactly how they are going to be victorious. They will vividly see themselves making birdie after birdie or touchdown after touchdown, so when the time comes to perform effectively their mind and body are fully prepared for the challenge. You can use this type of imagery to successfully conquer and accomplish any stressor or situation in your life. Before any major event, imagine yourself successfully rising to the challenge and accomplishing the challenge exactly how you want.

Meditation is another mental technique that you can use to manage stress. It is similar to mental imagery in that you are taking full control of the mind to adjust the way you are feeling. Meditation is very useful for people who are under heavy amounts of stress and for people who need to learn to relax effectively and reenergize themselves. Meditation involves focusing your mind on one thing for a continued period. During the course of this focusing, there should be no other thoughts that come into the mind. It will be very difficult at first to focus on only one thing for a continued period. In the beginning you may be able to focus correctly for one or two minutes before other thoughts begin to sneak in, but give it some time and eventually you will be able to maintain proper meditation for up to a half an hour or more. During meditation, you can focus on whatever you please as long as it is pleasant and it is only that one thing in particular. The object is to get everything else off your mind and train your brain to focus on one thing at a time. You can focus on things such as your breathing, sounds, a particular object such as a tree or flower, a favorite place, the sky, and anything else you may find interesting and relaxing. Whatever you choose it should be to your personal interest and liking. At the end of a long day, give yourself a few minutes a night to practice this until your concentration and focus are at your command. The more you improve at your meditation, the more you will learn the ability to relax your body and mind on command, even in the midst of your most difficult stressor.

Reducing the intensity of your reactions, emotionally and physically to stressors can help keep negative stress symptoms to a minimum, which is an overall aid in the process of stress management. When your stressors occur, try to make a conscious effort to minimize the intense feelings that would normally pass through your body. The majority of the time we are merely overreacting to our daily stressors. So, instead of overreacting to your stressor, try to make an effort to under-react to the stressor. When the situation occurs, ask yourself, *"What is the calmest most relaxed way I can react to this situation?"* Your brain will probably give you excellent feedback as to how to handle the situation properly and add some years to your life. When you begin to react to these stressors in a less intense manner you will begin to fear them less and less. Half the reason these stressors cause us so much anxiety is because we know how we normally react to them and how bad that reaction makes us feel. We then give the situation more importance than it really deserves. By adding more significance to the situation than it actually requires, we have no choice but to overreact to the stressor. Your mind cannot fear something that does not cause you uncomfortable feelings. Reacting to stressors in a relaxed manner will significantly diminish the fear and anxiety caused by life's difficult stressors.

Anger and frustration is another reaction that adds unneeded stress in your life. Implementing techniques to control and manage your anger can be very useful in reducing your daily stress. Here again, anger is a direct result to the way you react to particular stressors. The situation generally does not cause the anger, it is the hasty thoughts about the situation you let invade your mind that causes the anger. You can begin to manage your anger and frustration by admitting that you are angry at that particular moment in time. By admitting your anger, you can expect to react more frustrated, irritable, and irrational. When you are consciously aware of your anger, begin to analyze specifically what has caused the anger. Ask if the anger is necessary to the situation, and if you feel the anger is justified, ask yourself what is the best possible way of handling the situation. Many times when you realize exactly what is causing the anger, you may find it is causing you to put anger and frustrated feelings on other parts of your life. For example, you may have a day when you are extremely irritable toward everything your spouse has to say, when you begin to analyze why you are treating them this way, you may find there are problems bothering you at work or your dog may have eaten your new couch that morning. Instead of admitting the anger and facing it promptly, you may have attempted to finish the day assuming you would stay in good spirits. The technique of thought stopping can be a useful aid to control anger. When you become angry, think about the situation briefly and then consciously try to divert your attention away form it for the rest of the day. If the angry thoughts begin to pop up, promptly tell yourself to stop, and begin to think about something more pleasant. Being more flexible and understanding is another strategy that can be very useful in controlling your anger. Many people have very rigid views of how people should act around them and how situations turn out exactly according to their plan. These people want to have a major sense of control over everyone and every situation. Truth is, this is impossibility. You should not try to control external factors; you should only try to control the way you react internally to these external factors. If you can learn to understand people and their views a little better, you will learn to be a little more understanding when the situation does not go according to planned or when the individual does not behave as planned. By admitting your anger, analyzing your anger, using the thought stopping technique, and learning to become more flexible and understanding you can begin to properly control your daily anger. Remember, wood breaks because it is rigid; rubber bends because it is flexible. Do you want to break or bend?

Finding your optimal stress levels is a key ingredient in stress management. Life without any stress can be as detrimental as life with too much stress. We all perform our best when we are under a particular amount of stress. The amount of stress we thrive under will differ from person to person. However, the basics of optimal stress are the same for everyone. If we experience low amounts of stress in our life, we will begin to have feelings of boredom, low self-worth, and lethargy. I am sure retirees experience this quite often. If we high amounts of stress in our life we will begin to feel anxious, frustrated, unhappy, and fatigued. There is a happy median for everyone. You may experience optimal stress at times and totally be unaware that it was happening. There may have been days in your life that seemed to flow beautiful and you felt great all day. It is more than likely that you were thriving under your optimal stress level. During the days of optimal stress, you feel full of energy, that you can take on any challenge, that life is easy and fun, and that you will be a great success one day. You can find your optimal stress levels by monitoring your daily stress log. The days that were written in the log as feeling bored and unchallenged may have been a day of low stress. The days you feel over stressed, fatigued, helpless, and incompetent, may have been a day of high stress. The days you feel good are probably the days of optimal stress. Analyze the days you feel good to see how much stress was taking place. Some individuals optimal stress levels will be closer to the low end of stress and some individuals will thrive on the higher end of stress. When you begin to realize your optimal stress level, you can begin to restructure your life and try to reach that level of stress everyday. If your job requires a high amount of stress and you function well when you are at the lower end of stress levels, it may be time to search for a new career. Finding your optimal stress level will help you gain control over your life and catapult you into becoming an effective stress manager.

CONCLUSION

Stress management is a key puzzle piece to reaching total prosperity. When you begin to take charge of the stress in your life, you begin to gain more and more control of yourself and your daily decisions. Recognizing the symptoms of stress and the stress symptoms that you experience will allow you to gain a better understanding of what is causing the uncomfortable feelings. When you begin to consciously admit that you are under stress and that these stressors are causing your particular symptoms, you can begin the detailed search to find what in particular is causing your stress. Finding your daily life stressors and recognizing the symptoms each causes will allow you to begin a focused effort to control these stressors. To control stressors properly, you will need to take on the mindset of having a willingness to change. You will need to implement techniques such as drawing out a plan to manage stress, creating a daily stress log, learning to be mentally prepared for stress, using imagery and meditation, and reducing the intensity of your reactions to stressors. Another good stress management technique is learning to control your anger and frustration by admitting your anger, analyzing your anger, using mental thought stopping, and working to become more flexible and understanding. Understanding your optimal stress level is an excellent tool to use stress to your benefit. When you analyze you daily stress log, you will begin to find your optimal stress level. Knowing your optimal stress level will allow you to reach your maximum potential all day. Managing your daily stress will put more quality and control in your life; two things you will need a lot of to reach total prosperity. Taking control of your life piece by piece will allow you to understand that you control every feeling that passes through your body. Eventually the external world will never be able to control the way you feel.

*A person who controls their emotions
creates their own happiness!!*

Chapter 3

SPIRITUAL HEALTH

SPIRITUAL HEALTH IS AN IMPORTANT part of total prosperity. There are times in our lives when we have everything going in our favor but we never seem entirely happy, satisfied, or content about our lives. It is possible you could master other aspects of total prosperity and never reach a feeling of full happiness and prosperity if you cannot find spiritual health within. There are many people in this world who have everything going for them externally, they have a good job, they are nice looking, have a nice family, drive a nice car, etc... Often times, if you take a closer look something is missing in their lives. What is missing is a healthy spiritual life. These people, and it very well may be you I am speaking of, have become completely spiritually closed off. Their only thoughts in life are how to get ahead in the rat race, how to make more money, how to get more material possessions, how to look better, how to fit in with the crowd and so on and so on. These people become so involved with this delusional way of thinking that they will do anything to chase their mirage of empty goals and they will damage anything or anyone who gets in their way, including their own soul.

A person who lives a healthy spiritual life does not seek advice from the crowd for their own happiness; they do not gain their motivation from seeking power and material possessions, they simply want to live a life of happiness and have a feeling of positive successful fulfillment within themselves.

To learn to become a spiritually healthy individual, you must first understand that a healthy spiritual life involves the part of your life for which you cannot see. Spiritual health is the part of your life that involves your inner most being or your true self. When you are spiritually happy, everything else seems to work itself into place, you gain a sense of contentment and self-satisfaction about your life. Being spiritually happy will give you a sense of faith that even if things are not going well at the present moment in your life, it will eventually turn out the way you want it to.   Spiritual health is something that money cannot buy; it is completely unattainable through material possessions and power. When you learn to become a spiritually healthy person, it is something that no one will every be able to take away from you, whether rich or poor, rain or shine, you will always be able to take with you a spiritual wholeness that many will never be able to obtain.

Finding and maintaining your spiritual health is a major part of total prosperity, for when one is spiritually healthy, other pieces of the total prosperity puzzle will fall into place with the greatest of ease. It is hard to be miserable when you are in a healthy spiritual state and nothing externally affects your moods. The more spiritually open you become, the more your mind becomes open to new, more positive ideas about how to think and act.

Becoming a spiritually healthy individual will require you to grasp, understand, and master a series of simple thoughts and principles. These thoughts and principles are nothing new and you have probably heard them many times before. The difference this time is that you are going to gain a better understanding of each thought and principle and learn how to incorporate these thoughts and principles into your daily life. The spiritually healthy thoughts and principles that need to be master in order to reach spiritual health include: fully accepting yourself and your life; contentment; love; enjoying nature; keeping the heart of a child; gratitude; elevating your senses; faith; prayer; imagination; and taking full responsibility for your actions.

When you begin to implement these spiritual thoughts and principles into your life, you will find yourself growing increasingly internally peaceful and content with your life. Here again, positive changes will start to occur before your eyes. When you make the commitment to better your spiritual situation, you are making the commitment to rescue your life and the lives of the people around you who care and love you. The reason I say, "not only your life but also the lives of those around", is because when someone gains in spiritual health it becomes contagious and others crave to make the change in themselves that they see in you, and you will have the knowledge to show them how.

ACCEPTANCE

To become spiritually healthy you must first learn to fully accept yourself for who you are. When you can fully accept yourself for who you are, you will gain the ability to love your true individual self unconditionally. Now I do not mean to accept that you are lazy and sloppy and continue living in that manner happily, unless you are a pig. I simply mean to accept who you are presently, and make changes for the positive if necessary.

If you are an awkwardly built high school kid and do not like the way you look, simply learn to accept yourself for the way you presently look and seek out healthy, positive ways to improve your looks that may improve your self-image. If you are a single woman in the prime of your youth and are obese, learn to love yourself as is and work positively to do the necessary things it will take to improve your self-esteem. Now you may be thinking if I accept myself for who I am then why would I need to go seek means to change my appearance? You see it is possible to accept your present situation while improving on your future situation. The reason I want you to learn to fully accept your present situation is that the future is not guaranteed to any of us. Our present is all we have. For the corporate employee who is miserable in their job but continually thinks they will be much happier when their promotion comes, they are going to run in circles the rest of their life, because they can never accept their present situation. Shortly after their first promotion they find themselves to be unhappy wanting another promotion or job change, when it comes, they find the same unhappiness shortly after their arrival again and again.

If you are beginning to see a pattern in this book that many negative actions tend to work in cycles it is true. This poor corporate employee will live out the rest of their lives running this negative cycle just like a dog chasing his tail or better yet a hamster spinning his wheel, regardless, the result is the same, both end up exactly where they started gaining no ground at all. Spiritual health begins with acceptance of oneself and ones life. How can your soul ever be calm and grow healthy if you cannot accept your present self and situation?

The trick is, if you can learn to accept your present self and situations, you will gain a tremendous amount of self-esteem and self-efficacy, this increase in self-esteem and self-efficacy will enable you to more effectively better your future situations than the individuals who do not have full acceptance of their self and situations. There is no better peace mind than learning to fully accept yourself, accepting your weight, your hair, your eyes, the color of your skin, your nose, your complexion, your walk, your talk, your age, your scars, your past, your family, your job, your car, your residence, and everything else that is in your life. When you learn to accept the things in your life you will open up your soul for healthy spiritual growth, and you will stop running the hamster wheel.

Remember, fully accepting your present self and situation means you must fully accept everything that has happened in your life up until that point. Which includes your past and your family. If there are things that you have done in the past or others have done to you in the past, you must learn to put it behind you and accept it as part of your life and part of who you are. If there are family members that you have discrepancies with the things they have said and done to you or the way they live their life, you must let go of the anger and disappointment in these individuals and learn to acceptance them for who they are and what they have done, because they are part of your life and you cannot fully accept yourself without fully accepting every relative and every past occurrence in your life.

When total acceptance occurs in your life you will wonder how you ever managed to live without it. The tragedy is, there are many more people living without acceptance in their lives than people living with acceptance in their lives. By making a vow to learn to accept everything in your life, you will begin to grow spiritually and open up doors of opportunity you never knew existed.

CONTENTMENT

Once you learn to fully accept yourself, your past, and present life, you can begin to understand that spiritual health will require you to have a feeling of contentment in your life. By fully accepting who you are and where you have been, you are already reaching a form of contentment. When you can say, "I accept everything about myself ", you are telling yourself that you are content with who you are. This is the first step in becoming spiritually healthy.

To reach higher levels of spiritual growth, you must learn contentment in every aspect of your life. Being content in your current job, the spouse you are with, the place you live, and every little daily occurrence in your life. To learn full contentment you must gain an understanding that there is a higher power watching over all of us, and wherever we may be at that particular moment in time is exactly where we are meant to be, because are lives are being governed by a higher spiritual power. If you can take on the attitude that the job you are in right now, or the place you live right now, or who you are with, even if you are unhappy, is where you are supposed to be, you will gain a higher feeling of contentment.

When you gain in contentment, you begin to open new, positive doors in your life. If you can look at this particular place in your life and say, "hey, I'm here right now, it is where I am meant to be, even though I do not like it maybe I am supposed to learn something from this, I know it is only temporary, so I will be content with this situation and make the most of it."

I do not mean just taking this attitude with your job, love life, and financial situation, I mean taking it with every second of your life. The day you are running late and stuck in traffic is exactly where you are supposed to be at that particular moment, no you are not the unluckiest person in the world to get behind a dump truck and two school buses, it is merely where you are meant to be at that moment in time. Who knows, at our worst times someone may be looking out for our own well-being? If you had not been stuck in a traffic jam maybe there was a horrible accident waiting for further down the road. You must have a calm sense of contentment about every occurrence to reach a higher spiritual self.

Have you ever noticed that when you are happy and content with your personal place in life there always seems to be more opportunities coming your way? I remember a single friend of mine once told me that he never was looked at or hit on unless he felt content about himself and his life. The nights he was desperate and lonely, he would go out to the clubs with his friends to look for a date, and he would always come home empty handed, but when he was feeling confident and content about himself, he would get more dates and phone numbers than Johnny Depp. Now I cannot guarantee dates for every single person if they have a look of contentment in their eye, but I can guarantee they stand a better chance of finding a date over the individual who has a look of desperation and non-contentment in himself/herself.

Accompanying a strong sense of contentment is the relaxed attitude that everything is going to turn out just the way you want it to. This relaxed feeling is a direct correlation of being content. It is impossible to be content and unhappy at the same time and who would you think becomes more successful in life, the people that are happy, or the people that are unhappy?

LOVE

When you have learned contentment and full acceptance of yourself, your heart and mind should be open for new, healthy, and exciting feelings such as love. The love I speak of is truly a spiritually enhancing love. This love is a deep love based on respect and understanding. It is in the same category as the love you have for your parents, spouse, and children; it is just on a much broader spectrum. It is not just a love of individuals close to you; it is a love of all things on this Earth.

When you begin to grow spiritually, your mind begins to broaden and your eyes begin to see more clearly than they ever have before, giving you the ability to see things other than just your own unhappiness. When you acquire the understanding that it takes a strong person with a strong heart to give out love, and the more love you can give out the more love you will get in return, you will continue to grow in your new richly spiritual world.

Learning to love all things will require you to seek out the positive in every person you meet and every surrounding you encounter. When you begin to find the positive in these individuals and complement them on their positive qualities they in turn will begin to see the positive in you. Finding the positive in every surrounding you encounter will allow your heart to grow fond of that particular place whether good or bad.

Do you have the ability to drive past a nice park and find the love and beauty in it? You should be able to take the time and look at those beautiful trees and flowers in the park and find love in your heart for them. It should not take much effort for such beautiful creations. When you begin to give these wonderful creations love, you will begin to realize how magnificent they really are. Even a far worse person than your best friend or a far worse surrounding than a nice park, such as a mean in-law or your cubicle at work have at least one positive quality to put your focus on and give your love to.

Some things will require more effort to give love to, but be patient and if this person, place, or thing is difficult to find love in your heart for, you must seek out and focus only on there positive aspects even if it is only one. When you can focus on that one positive thing, you can create a more positive image for these people, places, or things.

However, there are certain exceptions to ever rule, and there are simply some people, places, and things in this world that have zero positive qualities about them other than being evil. My advice for these people, places, and things would be indifference instead of hate, and let the devil continue to give them his love. When you use hate, you drain your emotional energy; with indifference, you lose no emotional energy. With love, you gain emotional and spiritual energy, and when your heart begins to grow full of love, it is hard to harbor any negative feelings that may be detrimental to your spiritual health.

Learning to love on a broader spectrum will increase your spiritual energy, which in turn will create boundless new opportunities in your life. How can one ever grow spiritually rich without love in their life? Love is one of the strongest and positive emotions human beings will ever experience on Earth. Have you ever heard of someone who has too much of a loving spirit? If so I would like to meet him/her and spend some time with them, because a loving spirit is very contagious, and an encounter with these people always leaves you feeling refreshed. Learning to love all things on this Earth will create this positive loving spirit inside of you, which will become very prevalent to those around you.

Learning to love all things deeply and spiritually will give you respect and adoration from others, and when you gain respect and understanding from others, you will begin to respect and understand people, places, and things on a deeper spiritual level. This strong spiritual love will open your eyes to a new, more positive universe around you and you will then begin to understand yourself and your world around you on a much deeper level.

RESPECTING & ENJOYING NATURE

When your soul begins to grow and flourish you will begin to acquire a newfound respect for nature. As your soul begins to grow content and full of love, you begin to see things that you may have previously overlooked due to a state a discontentment, worry, anxiety, or unhappiness. When you begin to enjoy nature, you begin to respect nature. With the respect of nature comes a deeper understanding and requirement of patience within yourself that previously may not of existed.

While enjoying and respecting nature, you will begin to understand that it is amazingly alive. The tree in your back yard is alive just as you; it is a living functioning thing just as you. When you gain the awareness that all things in nature are alive, you can open your heart up to love these wonderful things that nature offers. Learn to love the squirrels, birds, chipmunks, raccoons, plants, trees, sky, and every other creation and creature nature has to offer.

When your soul is flourishing you can also find that nature has some breathtaking sights and sounds for your soul to see. Have you ever taken in a beautiful sunset and respected the beauty, mystery, and power of it? If you have not seen one lately, I recommend that you do. It can be very relaxing to the soul. Have you ever taken the time for your soul to take in the sound of a mountain stream or the rumble and spectacle of a thunder and lightning storm? Have you ever listened to the trees in a windstorm or simply watch the clouds pass by on a pretty day? Have you ever actually listened to birds singing or watched squirrels play together? If you have never experienced these amazing forces of nature, I recommend you make a point to start experiencing them right now. If you have experienced them, then I recommend that you make a point to continue doing so on a regular basis.

The more sights and sounds we are able to enjoy from nature, the more we will understand that we are not alone on this

Earth and that we should not be selfish with it. When you begin to open your eyes and look around at all the things nature holds, you will begin to see that we, as human beings, are merely a part of nature's process that represents a larger whole. The fact that we are the smartest species on this planet should make it our duty to protect and preserve all other things in nature to our fullest capabilities, not destroy them. The understanding is that we are a part of Mother Nature; Mother Nature is not a part of us.

For constant, strong spiritual growth, you should not let a day go by without taking a few minutes to see something beautiful that nature has to offer. Try to catch the sunset when you get home or the sunrise when you leave the house for work. Sit on your back porch or look out your window for something beautiful like the trees, birds, or small animals. Take in the beautiful sights and smells of flowers. Buy a plant or plant a garden and watch them grow from the hand of your care, work, and love. You can never have enough love and respect for nature.

The stronger your spiritual health grows, the stronger your love for nature will grow, and the stronger you love for nature grows the stronger your spirit will continue to grow. You see, positive traits tend to work in a cycle as well, only that get you somewhere in life.

KEEPING THE HEART OF A CHILD

Have you ever paid attention to the extreme happiness children tend to possess all throughout the day? Their innocent fun filled days seem to be immune to fears, worries, and anxieties. Can you remember the feelings you experienced when you were a child? I often think back to the things I did for fun when I was a child; the way I reacted to situations; and the vivid exploration of life I used to have.

One of the major differences I have noticed of an adult versus that of a child is the perception of how fast time passes by.

It seems once you reach a certain age in your life, which may vary from person to person, time passes by faster and faster. I like to equate the speed of time as one week in adult years passes by like one day in child days. I can remember when I was a child and each day of my life would seem to last forever. Children have a way a getting the full potential out of each day of their lives.

Child like positive qualities tend to dissipate one by one as we reach adulthood. Children have a blind innocence about them, which leaves them going into every situation free from disabling fear and preconceptions of what might happen. On the road to adulthood, this child like quality tends to disappear. From whatever negative occurrences they have seen or experienced in their lives, it eventually strips the blind innocence away, where the result of every new situation has a preconceived outcome to it. For example, let's take a young woman who has been hurt in a past relationship years ago, in her present life she has met a wonderful man that she is having deep feelings for, instead of approaching this relationship with a blind innocence and mystery of where the relationship will go, she is more than likely saying things to herself such as, "I really like this guy, but I know he is just going to hurt me in the long run", or "even if this goes good I'll probably do the same thing I did in the past relationship that made it go bad." When you begin to focus on thoughts as these, due to letting your blind innocence fade, they will eventually self-destruct your success in the most important aspects of your present and future life, including your spiritual, personal, and financial success.

It is possible to teach yourself to go into all situations, regardless of how awful past experiences have been, and have a blind innocence, without any judgment of the situations future outcome, due to your past shortcomings. This can be done because the reality of life is that each day is a new day and because something bad happened to you yesterday does not mean something bad is going to happen to you today.

Children also have a curiosity quality about them, which is another reason time appears to move slower for them. Children can go outside and play all day without ever getting bored. They can go in the woods or play in creek for hours, exploring all the wonderful mysteries our world has to offer. The reason they have the ability to entertain themselves so efficiently is that they have vivid imaginations, and that they have no preconceived notions of what is out their waiting on them. Here again, as we enter into adulthood our imagination has a tendency to fade, and we begin to preconceive more and more of life's mysteries. Preconceived notions cause us to assume the result before it has actually occurred, just as you have a preconceived notion of what an apple taste like before you eat it, which keeps you from enjoying it's full flavor.

When you were a child you could run through the woods and pretend you were a super hero trying to save the world, you were free from all of life's worries, especially time, if you came across an abandoned shed, your imagination would begin to run wild with thoughts of the limitless opportunities this shed could bring you and the wonderful treasures that lie inside. When you are an adult, the thought of running through the woods is probably not that appealing anymore. Even though it would probably get your mind off your worries. Even by a slight chance if you were to imagine you were a superhero without the help of narcotics or alcohol, you would probably think you need psychiatric help, and as for coming across an abandoned shed, you would probably pass right by it, because you have seen them in the woods before your whole life and your preconception tells you there is probably nothing to it or nothing in it, but how do you really know nothing is in it? Who is to say there is not something of value lying inside?

If you make it a goal in life to get your positive child like qualities back, you will find many new opportunities in the process. The first child like quality to regain is letting go of all your preconceptions. If you do not let go of your preconceptions, your life will just become a daily carbon copy of that particular day the week before, because you have created preconceptions for everything in your life for every second of your life. When this occurs and you cannot decipher one week from the next is when time really begins to fly by.

To stop this and break out of your preconceptions, you have teach yourself to look and experience everything in your life, and I mean everything, as if it were the first time you were experiencing it. Only then will you be able to slow the clock down and gain more qualities you had as a child; and believe me, as a whole, children have more qualities that induce happiness than adults. The more qualities you have that induce happiness, the more you will find yourself living the good life and your spiritual health growing strong.

GRATITUDE

Showing gratitude for all the things in your life is an excellent way to improve your spiritual health. Having gratitude involves a state of mind that includes becoming thankful and appreciative of everything and everyone in your life. The best way to finding true spiritual peace and happiness is to focus on all the things that you have, and try not to focus on all the things that you do not have. If you notice, the majority of humans are trained to live their entire life trying to acquire things they do not have. When they acquire the possession they did not previously have, they simply begin the soul devouring cycle over again to chase down their next possession. Their possession can be anything; a new car, a new house, a new job, a new look, a new husband or wife, a new town to live in, etc... The reason I call it a soul devouring cycle is that the majority of humans completely forget all of the good things they already posses while they are on the quest for their next possession, and they end up living a completely empty life only knowing of the next possession they must acquire to feel whole, never finding true happiness.

From day one it is as if we are taught to go to school; go to a good college; get a good job, regardless if you like it or not; and start playing the game. What is the game? The game is that internal program we have been taught that tells you that you should be making this amount of money at such and such age, and married by this age, and buying your first house by this age, and your 401K should look like this by this age, and you should be driving this type of car by this age, and you should be dressing and acting like this by this particular age, and so on and so on. I do not know why our system seems to instill this program in us, but maybe that is not for us to know. The point is not where or why we learned it, but how to unlearn this and become grateful of all things in our life.

The first step to learned gratefulness is to stop focusing on the things you do not have in your life. Can you guess the second step? It is to start focusing on all the things that you do have, things such as your health, job, house, spouse, children, faith, car, clothes, the food on your table, the ability to move and breathe, your five senses, being alive, and everything else that is a part of your life. You see, when you begin to put your attention on all the things you already have, a feeling of gratefulness begins to come upon you, and you begin to realize how well you already have it. Now I am not telling you to just sit still and not chase any of your dreams. I am just telling you that in the process of chasing those dreams consistently focus on the things you already have in your life.

When you are feeling grateful about your life, your spirit can flourish and continue to grow. When your spirit is growing healthy, it becomes much easier to obtain your goals and dreams. The individual who does not see it this way continues along in a state of consistent state of unhappiness and emptiness. The cause of this emptiness and unhappiness is due to constant consumption. These individuals consume all things in their path to try to fill the void of their ungratefulness. In their minds, they have nothing to be grateful for in their lives, but if they obtain their next possession, that will make them very grateful and happy. This chasing and illusion of ungratefulness will continue for the rest of their lives until the end.

It sounds miserable, but it is reality for a great many of us humans. The only way for it to stop is to teach yourself to be grateful of everything little thing that comes your way. You will have to fight greed, jealousy, envy, and especially the tendency of wanting to be like everyone else. If you cannot fight the tendency of waning to follow the trends, you will find yourself back in the pattern of doing and wanting everything your friends, piers, and colleagues are doing and wanting. This will lead you right back to the empty quest for your next possession with no consideration of your present possessions, and your present possessions is all you truly have. While you are in the process of reaching your own personal goals and dreams, *not anyone else's goals and dreams*, remember to focus on the things you already have, this allow your spiritual health to continue growing.

ELEVATING YOUR SENSES

Becoming aware of your senses and heightening them to a new level is an excellent way to increase your spiritual health. Taking time out in your hectic life to enjoy the simple things you were given is a great way to start enjoying life to its fullest.

The older we get and the busier we become in life, we seem to lose the awesome power of our senses and use them only when required, never tapping their full potential again. How many beautiful sunsets have you driven by lately without giving it a second glance? How many great meals have you simply wolfed down without enjoying the true flavor fully? When is the last time you listened to the wonderful sounds of nature or enjoyed a good song? Have you used your sense of touch lately and felt the softness of your wife's back or the feel of water splashing on your face? When have you taken the time to stop and smell the beautiful aroma of a flower garden? These questions are to remind you that you do have five wonderful senses and they were given to you for a reason, and I am quite certain the reason they were given to us was not to ignore them or take them for granite everyday. I would like to believe the reason we were given these great senses is to use them to their fullest capabilities so we can enjoy a better life.

When you make a conscious effort to elevate your senses and use them to their fullest potential you begin to experience many amazingly simple things that often go overlooked. Experiencing these simple things in life, which do not cost a thing, will increase your spiritual health ten fold. All you have to do is slow down and take the time to see, smell, hear, taste, and touch all the treasures that life has to offer you. I can tell you from experience there is a boundless, endless supply of treasures for you to unveil.

You can begin to elevate your senses by simply sitting down at your next meal, and instead of taking it for granite, let your sense of taste take over. Do not think of anything else but how the food and drink taste. Savor every bite as if it were your last. Then if you seemed to enjoy that meal more than your previous meals, try to elevate your other senses by taking the time to enjoy the sounds, smells, and sights nature has to offer. Before you know it, you will begin to feel more alive than you ever have before. When you stop and take the time to elevate your senses, you will begin to feel as if you have awakened from a deep sleep, and this awakening will allow your spiritual health to continue growing.

FAITH

Faith is the essence of spiritual health. *Webster's* has a few definitions of faith which include: allegiance; belief and trust in God; confidence. When talking about faith I will try to make my points of the importance of faith without mentioning religion, so I do not offend anyone or leave anyone out. I know there are many different religions and many of them contradicting to each other. Nevertheless, the fact of the matter is, who or whatever you believe in, you should have faith in that. If you do not like the religion you are currently end, then I recommend that you find one you can gain faith in. If you are an atheist, I cannot offer much advice, but I would suggest that you find some outside force to put your allegiance in. Having a strong sense of faith in a higher force can bring a great sense of meaning and serenity in your life. By the definition above, there are several positive words to focus on when we are talking about faith.

The first is allegiance, when you have an allegiance with something, you have a friend or an ally, and in today's world with modern day pressures, you cannot have enough friends or ally's. The next two positive words are belief and trust; these are both positive words because they represent affirmation in something. To become spiritually healthy it is more than just believing and trusting in a higher force, it is believing and trusting in the fact that this higher force has your best interest at hand. You must trust that even if things are going bad now, they will eventually turn out positive, because the God in which you believe loves you and has a good life prepared for you, there are just difficult test times along the way. The last positive word is confidence. When you have a strong faith in your God, and you know in your heart that your God is good and that your God loves you. You can then gain a sense of confidence over those who do not have a strong sense of faith. This supreme confidence can only be found in deep sense of faith, and when you experience it, it can be one of the most powerful feelings that you ever feel.

To begin increasing your faith, I recommend you start practicing your religion, go to a spiritual place that preaches your religion, if you do not already, and read as much literature about your faith as often as you possible can. The more you stay focused on your faith the stronger and confident you will become. Having faith in your beliefs will help you affirm, trust, and have confidence that you are headed in a positive direction and that you truly deserve to live a good life. This affirmation in yourself and your life, coming from an increase in faith, will allow your spiritual health to continue to thrive and grow.

PRAYER

Using prayer in your life is another great way to grow spiritually. It is also an excellent way to reduce stress, worry, and anxiety in you life. It is important to understand that prayer does not work unless you have Faith. When you gain a strong faith in you beliefs, you can begin to use prayer as another positive faction in your life. You can begin to pray for yourself and others happiness, health, success, love, courage, strength, and piece of mind. When you have faith that these prayers will be answered, your life will begin to gravitate in the direction of your prayers.

The key to good prayer is to believe in your heart that someone is actually listening and answering your prayers. This is something that is not hard to learn, and if you already pray, I recommend you that you continue praying for the rest of your life, if you do not pray I recommend that you start today. Prayer can be very habit forming all you have to do is start. Try to make a pact with yourself to start out by saying a small prayer as you lay down for bed. When you lay down, you can start your prayer, it does not have to be aloud, you can say it to yourself, and begin to ask for the good things you want for and out of yourself and others. When this evening prayer becomes a habit, you can begin a morning prayer when you wake up to get the day started on a positive note. I am not going to tell you anymore how to pray, or when to pray, because I believe prayer is very personal, it is something that should be from the heart, and whenever you want to do it. I am simply trying to give guidelines and aid those individuals who are in the dark when it comes to praying. I will say this, prayer is a definite positive in anyone's life, and I recommend it to all.

When you pray, you are creating a personal one-on-one relationship with the God you have faith in and worship. Anytime you can create a personal relationship and allegiance with a higher power, great things will come into your life. I often feel sorry for individuals who think they can live a truly happy and successful life without guidance from above, and you would be surprised how people there are who think they can. For your spirit to grow healthy, you will need to incorporate positive spiritual prayer in you life on a daily basis.

IMAGINATION

The use of a vivid imagination has created many great individuals and these individuals have created many great things. Do you believe you could be one of these special, creative individuals? Well you can, all you have to do is keep your imagination running high and running positively.

Many people use their imagination more than they realize, the only problem is these individuals are imagining horribly negative things in their life. Often when we worry about things it is merely our imagination running high, it is just focused on the negative. The type of imagination I want you to master is slightly different than the type of imagination I mentioned in children. Children's imagination is based highly on curiosity and innocence, although this is a great type of imagination and I would like everyone to try keeping a large part of that in them, so they can still have the ability as adults to run through the woods pretending they are some type of super hero. It is also very fun, it is an excellent stress and anxiety killer, there is nothing wrong with it, and it is a great escape from your everyday problems.

The type of imagination I am speaking of is slightly different. There are good and bad types of it, and the bad type can be very common in adults. The positive type is an imagination of the positive, it is a trait rarely found in the average individual and common in successful individuals. To become spiritually healthy, this positive imagination is something that needs to be implemented your life on a daily basis. The problem is, for some reason or another, we as humans find it far less difficult to find ourselves imagining negative thoughts instead of positive thoughts. Questioning negative imaginative thoughts like, what would happen if, I lose my Job? What would happen if my wife leaves me and takes the kids? What would I do if my parents were to pass away? What if I never get promoted? How would I pay my mortgage next month if I did not get my commissions? What if the stock market crashed? The negative questions that we continuously put through our minds are nothing more than a vivid imagination only slanted negatively. The good news here is that we still have imaginations; the bad news is the majority of us use them negatively.

Need not worry, it can be repaired, all you have to do is work to angle your imagination to the positive. When negative imaginative thoughts come into your mind, you must tell yourself to STOP thinking that and think of something positive. You need to get in the habit of replacing every negative imaginative thought that comes to your mind with a positive imaginative thought. An imaginative thought is anything that has not occurred in your life up until this very moment, for example; any thoughts you have about your life next week is imaginative, because it is not physically here in the present. The key is to make these imaginative thoughts positive, exaggerate them if you have to. It is funny how the negative imaginative questions above are taken far more serious than positive imaginative questions like, what if I become CEO of this company one day? What if I wrote an inspirational book? What if my parents around for my entire life? What if my wife and kids love me more than anything on this planet? What if a major firm wants to hire me? What would I do if I had the power of company Vice President? How would I feel if I ran a marathon? What if the value of the stock market went straight to the top? These imaginative questions probably make you laugh and say *yea right* to yourself, without ever giving them another thought. However, the negative thoughts leave you feeling low and have you giving serious thought and consideration about would happen if these horrible things were actually to occur. The sad irony here is that we should be doing the exact opposite of what we are doing. The positive imagination is what we should give serious thought and consideration to, and the negative is what we should laugh off and give no serious thought and consideration to.

Our imaginations are extremely powerful, and that what we focus on and imagine we tend to gravitate towards. You need to pay attention and understand how often you actually use your imagination, and make any positive corrections that a necessary. Keep in mind that you are better off with no imagination at all than to have a negative imagination. When you posses a positive imagination, you posses an unseen powerful force that will keep you leaps and bounds ahead of those who cannot imagine positively. Imagining positively is no magic trick; the ones who cannot imagine positively are simply those who have never read this and do not understand that they are using their own imagination destructively.

For your spiritual health to grow strong, you have to keep your mind and especially your daily imagination in the positive world. It is virtually impossible to have good spiritual health without a positive imagination. Here again, it becomes a positive, giant snowball affect, the more your positive imagination increases, the more your spirit grows, and the more your spirit grows the more your positive imagination will grow.

TAKING RESPONSIBILITY FOR YOUR ACTIONS

True Spiritual health will require you to take full responsibility for your actions. There comes a point in all of our lives when we understand right from wrong, good from bad, and lazy from determined. The sooner you are able to understand this the better. At this point in your life, you have to realize that anything you do from that moment on is a direct reflection on you. The moment you understand this, you cannot put blame on anyone for how bad your life is and how bad it is going to be, because you now know what it takes to live the god life and you have the ability to change matters. I think I gained my complete understanding when I was around 17 years old. I found that I had been feeling sorry for myself, and the negative things I had been through up until that point. I was doing a lot a blaming and finger pointing for my problems, at that moment I realized I knew many adults that were close to me who blamed all their past mistakes on an unfortunate upbringing and unfortunate negative past occurrences, and I always got upset watching these adults constantly self destruct because they had a built in failure mechanism due to their perception of their upbringing or unfortunate past occurrences, and they could always blame their failures on that. It used to drive me crazy watching this occur, yet I found myself following the same exact pattern, at that precise moment I looked in the mirror at myself and I told myself that I was old enough now that I knew right from wrong and I knew what it took to fail in life or succeed in life and whatever I did from that moment on was no one else's fault but my one. At that moment, I decided to take full responsibility for my own life and it was a liberating experience. I could feel my spirit grow stronger as a put life on my shoulders and stopped pointing fingers for my feeling low and the bad things that had occurred in my life. I was fortunate enough to have a spiritual experience like that to bring me an awareness of my built failure mechanism. At that moment, I was able to destroy it and it has never existed again in my life.

The sad truth is many are never fortunate enough to have an experience like that; they just go on self-destructing because they feel they can put the blame of failure on to someone else. The kids who live a life in and out of prison because their father was a criminal and it is his fault they decided to commit a felony; The abusive parent who blames their poor parenting skills on their alcoholic father, when in fact it is they who are physically and mentally abusing their own children, not the alcoholic grandfather; the alcoholic and drug abuser who blames his addictions on his wife leaving him, when in fact he is the one who abuses the drugs and puts the drinks down day after day not her. Do you see the pattern? The pattern is that they are all adults who know right from wrong and they are blaming someone else for their problems. The pattern continues with them destroying themselves, destroying others, or both. This is a horrible pattern for these individuals and for those around them that care. The only way to set yourself free is to break out of your failure mechanisms and take full responsibility for all your actions.

If you find yourself blaming anyone for any of your problems, you should take a moment to check yourself and realize there is only one person to blame, and that person is the one who Stares back at you when you look in the mirror. When the vow is made to take full responsibility for your life, you will be making a statement of strong independence, throwing your failure mechanisms away and walking on your own, and your spiritual health will grow stronger with you every step of the way. It is pure freedom.

CONCLUSION

Learning to live a spiritually healthy life through these eleven thoughts and principles will be a journey that will require you to look back on your life, analyze your present life, and make the necessary changes for your future life. When you begin to look back on your life you can find the times of your peak happiness and sadness, analyzing the causes of each. You can analyze your present life to see what changes can be made in your daily routine to better your spiritual situation. You can then set a positive spiritual plan for your future.

When these eleven thoughts, feelings, and principles are implemented into your life, your entire world, as you know it, will begin to change right before your very eyes. These thoughts and principles are designed to change your spiritual world and to show you what it feels like to be truly alive. We can have all the things life has to offer, but without spiritual health, they are nothing more than hollow possessions. If spiritual health is something that no amount of money can buy, and no material possession can replace, you should put your emphasis on making sure you are spiritually healthy before you do anything else. When you make spiritual health a priority, everything else such as happiness, wealth, and relationships, will fall more easily into place. With a calm, content, and strong spirit, a person can exceed their greatest dreams.

You can achieve this by practicing these eleven principles until they are a part of your life. Each principle is a helpful part of reaching spiritual health, but they all work better when used together. Each principle has a parts to it that make other principles stronger when used together, such as acceptance and love; respecting nature and elevating your senses; faith and prayer. Try to use your self-discipline by not letting a day go by from this moment on without incorporating these principles into your life. You can start by mastering one, for with one the others will follow, or you can try to use all of them throughout the course of the day. Either way you choose it does not matter, as long as you begin practicing them on a daily basis until they become second nature. In the process of mastering these principles, be prepared to feel more alive than you ever have, it is what they call spiritual health!

Get busy living or get busy dying!!

Chapter 4

FRAME OF MIND

TO BECOME AN INDIVIDUAL WHO possess total prosperity it is mandatory that you maintain a positive frame of mind throughout each day of your life. Your overall frame of mind is key factor to your overall success. Individuals who posses a positive frame of mind accomplish most all of their goals and win in most all of their situations. By win, I mean they will when in most situations where others will fail, which allows them to win the ultimate game called life. They are the ones who have the most happiness, the most friends, the most money, and the most of their wants and needs. They very rarely will lack in any area of their life, and if they did, they would find a way to gain what they are lacking. They will do anything to protect and maintain their positive frame of mind.

It should come as no big surprise that the individuals with the most positive frame of mind win. When we are talking about frame of mind, we are talking about the way you feel about yourself, your life, your opportunities, your accomplishments, and the control you feel you have over the success of your life. These are all extremely important and are directly related to your success. How you feel about yourself is a direct result of the image you feel you are portraying to others. How you feel about your life, your opportunities, and your control is a direct result of your happiness. In essence, your frame of mind is a mirror image of the life you have lived, currently live and will live in the future. I hope it is becoming apparent why the individual's with the most positive mind frames win in life.

An individual's frame of mind is comparable to the frame of a house. The houses with the strongest frames are more in value, more in demand, and they can withstand more adversity than ones with the weaker frames. The individuals with the strongest, positive frame of mind are thought of in the same light. They are more in demand, which makes them more valued, and they can withstand more adversity, which makes them stronger than the individual's who have a weaker frame of mind.

If your frame of mind is the base or structure from which your life is built upon, it is something that should have a lot of care and concern placed upon it. Your frame of mind is something that cannot be taken for granite or go overlooked. It is something that must be restructured and mastered for you to reach total prosperity. The restructuring of your frame of mind begins by focusing on changing your negative frame of mind or sometimes slightly positive frame of mind to a *Complete, Continuous, and Constant* positive frame of mind.

I put emphasis on *complete, continuous, and constant*. You see, many people have a good frame of mind some of the time, and they have a good frame of mind about certain areas of their life while having a negative frame of mind in other areas of their life. Others or sadly, the majority of people, have a negative frame of mind most all of the time. When you properly restructure your frame of mind, you will have a *Complete* positive frame of mind, where you keep a positive mind frame about every aspect of your life. You will also have a *Constant* and *Continuous* positive frame of mind, where you feel positive not just some of the time or never, but all the time. When you begin to gain a complete and constant positive frame of mind, it becomes addictive and you will do anything to keep it, including destroying every negative in your life, wherever it may lie.

Restructuring your frame of mind to the positive will require you to gain an understanding and enlightenment in a series of thoughts and principles, just as you did to improve your spiritual health. These restructuring thoughts and principles will coincide with other thoughts and principles you have already learned in spiritual health. They will in turn increase the magnitude of the positive impact each thought and principle will have on your life. The thoughts and principles for positive spiritual health and the thoughts and principles for positive frame of mind will work together as a team to bring your life into a positive realm and bring you closer to total prosperity.

The thoughts and principles used to restructure your frame of mind to the positive include; conscious awareness of your frame of mind; deserving; internally controlled; living in the moment; you attract what you give; perception is reality; recognizing personal problems; dedication; search for inspiration; avoiding the media; and questioning everything. When these thoughts and principles are implemented into your life, your frame of mind will begin to restructure itself to become more positive. You will then begin to be one of the lucky and envied ones who win the game!

CONCSIOUS AWARENESS OF YOUR FRAME OF MIND

To become an individual who possess a positive frame of mind, you must first become consciously aware that you do have a frame of mind and it controls a big part of your life. Your frame of mind is an inner feeling and an inner voice that tells you things such as, how you feel about yourself, and how much financial and spiritual happiness you believe you will have. This inner voice and inner feeling is one of the most important aspects of your life. If you were a computer, your frame of mind would be your hard drive. When your frame of mind is functioning properly, unconquerable obstacles do not exist. When your frame of mind is not functioning properly, your minds eye feels as if there are unconquerable obstacles around every corner.

Becoming consciously aware of your frame of mind will allow you to understand what it is causing your positive and negative mind frames. To become consciously aware of your mind frame you must begin to listen within. Listening within will require you to pay close attention to every daily thought that passes through your mind. This may seem a little difficult at first, but once you have trained your brain to become consciously aware of your thought pattern, you will be able to realize if your frame of mind is functioning more positively or more negatively.

To break out of the negative and have your frame of mind function properly and positively you will require you to begin listening to this inner voice and inner feeling that make up your frame of mind. You will have to listen to your self-conscious or inner self, because that is where the structure and blueprint of your frame of mind lies. Listen to what you are thinking every second of the day. Is it negative? Is it positive? Are these thoughts moving you toward a future goal? Is what I you are thinking causing you to progress or regress? The answers to these questions may come as a surprise to you. You will also need to pay attention to every daily inner feeling you experience. Are these feelings mainly positive or negative? How do these feelings affect your emotions? Are these feelings creating a better life for you or are they making your life worse? Gaining a conscious awareness of your frame of mind will allow you to clearly hear and feel these thoughts and feelings. It will give you the ability to ask yourself proper questions, which will aid in the understanding of the direction these inner thoughts and feelings are taking you.

When you have reached a conscious awareness and gain the ability to listen and question your inner voice and inner feelings, you can then begin to ask yourself the most important question about the state of your frame of mind; WHY. The question WHY, will begin to lead you in a direction of positive restructuring. Restructuring questioning such as, why am I thinking and feeling negatively? What has or is causing the negative feelings in my frame of mind? Why is my frame of mind leaving me feeling frustrated? What can I do to stop the negative thoughts and feelings? Why or what is causing me to have positive days? What can I do to have more positive than negative days in my life? How can I have a consistent, constant, and continuous positive frame of mind? The WHY questioning will lead you down a road of better understanding within. You will gain a conscious understanding of the causes of your happiness and sadness.

To make any positive change in your life you have to understand and ask yourself questions of where, why, and how the negative took up residence and began to feel comfortable in your life. These are very legitimate questions because negative thoughts, habits, and living should not feel comfortable in your life. Unfortunately, the most people do not see it that way and living in the negative is a way of life, it is comfortable in their lives.

When you become consciously aware of your frame of mind, you will begin to understand that the negative in your life is not natural and should not be made to feel comfortable in your life. When you ask yourself questions such as, how does feeling negative all day make me feel? Am I more productive when I think negative or when I think positive? Did I enjoy the day more when I think positive or when I think negative? Do I feel healthier when I think positive or negative? I will bet you felt better; were more productive; and enjoyed the days more when you were thinking positive. The reason being is that a negative frame of mind is not natural to us, and our mind and bodies will reject anything that is not natural. Just as anyone will cough when they inhale a cigarette for the first time, there bodies reject it, but after inhaling enough of them their body and mind grow used to it, even though it is slowly killing them; just as cigarette, so many people grow used to the negative in their lives, even though it is slowly killing them.

When you gain a conscious awareness of your frame of mind, which consist of your inner voice and feelings. You will begin to hear the voices and thoughts within yourself that would have previously gone overlooked without conscious recognition. These thoughts and voices may surprise you as to how negative they are, but when you begin to understand them properly, you will begin to understand where the negative is hiding itself in your life, just as a snake hiding in the grass. When you gain a conscious understanding of where the negative is hiding in your life, you will then be able to destroy it.

When the negative begins to dissipate in your life you will begin to understand that it is completely natural for us to live positive lives. Living with a positive frame of mind will make you feel like an entirely different person than living in the negative. You will feel more alive, more energetic, more focused, more productive, more rested, more creative, and much healthier. You will then gain a conscious understanding that negative in your life is not natural and the reason it was making you feel lousy was that your body and mind were trying to resist it. Knowing this will allow you to spit the negative cigarettes out of your life and take a positive breath of fresh air.

DESERVING

An individual who possess a positive frame of mind believes in their heart that they are deserving of that positive frame of mind. They believe that they are deserving of living the good life. The reason I make this point is that many individuals who posses a negative frame of mind cannot handle or maintain for any descent period of time, any type of prosperity in their lives. The reason being is that when prosperity occurs, they simply feel that they are non-deserving and eventually self-destruct against the prosperity that has occurred.

This feeling of non-deserving can have a very detrimental affect on ones life if they do not change their thought pattern. The fact is if you have understood the power of faith, then you should understand that we are destined and deserving of good and prosperous things to occur in our lives. The hardest part of learning to feel deserving of prosperity will be convincing yourself that you truly are. A feeling of deserving is simply a content feeling within yourself that you have truly earned the right to feel happy and have such wonderful prosperity in you life.

It sounds simply, but you would be surprised as to how many people do not feel this way, and how many people there are that do not understand the importance of feeling deserving of prosperity. Feeling deserving of prosperity is a key ingredient to a properly functioning frame of mind. For without it, you will only end up with what you feel you deserve. Most of the time, the individuals who feel they do not deserve prosperity, also feel they do not deserve happiness in their life. When you do not feel you deserve happiness in life, you might as well stick a fork in yourself, because you are truly done for. Do you know what a feeling of non-deserving of happiness produces? It is simple; it produces no happiness and a lot or misery.

We all know the individuals I am speaking of that cannot hold on to happiness or prosperity. When happiness is occurring in their lives, they simply say, " I cannot believe I feel this happy, it should be a crime to feel this good." "Something must be wrong, I should not feel this good, I am usually worrying at this time of day." "If I feel this good now, that means something bad is going to happen to take my happiness away." On prosperity, "How did a person like me meet someone so wonderful?" "Are they hiding something from me?" "How could my boss possibly want to promote me over my more educated co-worker?" "How did I land this great job, something must be wrong?" These self-destructing questions will cause these unfortunate individuals to subconsciously ruin whatever happiness and prosperity they encounter. The reason being is that deep in their inner self, they do not possess a true deserving frame of mind. If you have ever experienced anything similar to these self-defeating questions, you may be in the midst of a non-deserving frame of mind and it will be time to change this thought pattern.

An individual with a deserving frame of mind would have an entirely different internal response to happiness and prosperity. It would be more like, "I love feeling this happy, and this is what I am supposed to feel like all the time!" "I am a little lethargic, usually I feel very enthused this time of day, let me see if I can get that feeling back." "I deserve to feel this good for the rest of my life." On prosperity, " This person is a wonderful asset in my life, I always knew I would meet someone this wonderful." "I had a feeling my boss thought I was the man for the job, even if my co-worker was more educated." "I knew I was going to get this job, I deserve it!" The deserving individual has an entirely different set of internal responses to happiness and prosperity. These different internal responses to happiness and prosperity allow them to have and maintain happiness and prosperity for a lifetime.

An individual with a deserving frame of mind expects to be happy and prosperous. When you expect to be happy and prosperous, your life has a tendency to become happy and prosperous. All you have to do is expect any happiness or prosperity that occurs in your life. Do not over analyze the happiness and prosperity, just welcome it into your life and realize that you deserve it. Gain the understanding that you are supposed to be happy and prosperous, and unhappiness is not welcome in your life. We all deserve to live the good life filled with happiness and prosperity.

Do you see where this is going? The person you are and everything you possess up until this point is everything you feel you deserve, because if you sincerely felt you deserved better, then it would be. You see we have the power as human beings to obtain anything we put our minds to, and when we feel we deserve better than what we have, our minds begin to gravitate in the direction of the better things we feel we deserve. With this in mind, you need to understand the importance of deserving notions. If you feel you deserve a positive frame of mind and it is your right to be happy and prosperous then it will become a reality.

INTERNAL CONTROL

To acquire excellence with your frame of mind will require you to gain a sense of internal control over your life. When internal control is mastered, the condition of your daily frame of mind will be entirely up to you. The weather, the people around, your job, the government, your children, and the economy will not be able to push your frame of mind into the negative. Internal control involves an understanding that you are in control of your feelings and nothing, not anyone or anything, can affect them. The only thing that affects your frame of mind and feelings is the way you let yourself react to certain situations. Just think about, if your wife or boss says things that upset and demean you, it is not the words from their tongue that hurt you, instead it is the thoughts you let go through your mind about those words that hurt you.

Your thoughts are very alive, and every thought you think tells your body and frame of mind how to feel. Therefore, our thoughts greatly affect our feelings. If your boss or wife is demeaning, and it is upsetting, you are the one thinking, "Why do they say such hurtful things"? "Don't they know how bad this makes me feel"? "What if I really am these things they are saying"? By the time it is all said and done, you are feeling miserable and you are telling yourself that it is their fault for doing it. The fact is, if it is truly their fault for making you feel unhappy, you might as well be a puppet on a string with absolutely zero control over your life. The good news is, this is far from the truth, the bad new is, most individuals do not believe the good news.

An individual who has gained the understanding of internal control has the ability to restructure their thoughts in the midst of a crisis against their frame of mind. If a boss or spouse were trying to upset them with abusive words, they would simply tell themselves, "I do not need to pay attention to this, they are just upset and do not know how to communicate effectively, it is no slight against me." "I will not let these words make me feel any less great than I do right now." "If they want me to change, I can work on it, but they will have to change the way they speak to me first." When the conversation is over, the internally controlled individual feels no different. They realize the importance of every thought that passes through their mind, and the importance of how these thoughts affect their feelings.

Again, your thoughts are alive. Your thoughts affect your feelings. Your feelings affect your frame of mind. Who has control over your thoughts? I hope you did not say your spouse or your boss. Who controls your feelings? Please say it is you, and not, "it depends on which way the wind is blowing." You are the only one who has control over what you are thinking; it is purely your choice.

Whatever thought goes in your mind will produce a feeling, maybe not immediately, but mark my words, it will produce a feeling before it is over. No thought goes through your mind without producing some type of reaction or feeling. So, if things circumstances begin to attack your positive frame of mind and you cannot find positive thoughts, make an effort to think nothing at all. You are better off walking around all day thinking nothing at all like a mindless zombie, than thinking negative. At least you will be in neutral and not reverse, because when you are thinking negatively, you might as well be in a car going in reverse over a mountain, into the valley of misery.

When you are allowing only positive thoughts to enter in to your mind, you will be moving forward in life headed in a positive direction. Understand that you are the only one who controls your world. There is nothing externally that can affect your frame of mind, not the negative things you see, what you hear, what you look like, what others are doing, or your job. The only thing that can affect your frame of mind is what you choose to think. With this is mind, you had better make sure your what you are allowing to enter your mind is only positive thoughts. The fact of the matter is you control your life. You control you happiness, your sadness, and your prosperity, every aspect of your life is directly controlled by you. The amount of money you make, the type of spouse you have or will have, where you live, the car you drive, and your hobbies, are all your doing. It is a simple way of thinking, your world is controlled from the inside, and you control it all. I said, you control it all; you control it all; you control it all!

LIVING IN THE MOMENT

To maintain a positive frame of mind it is imperative that you train yourself to live life in the present moment. Savoring every second of your life accomplishing all that you will without any sluggish thoughts of regret or worry. An excellent role model is Mother Nature. You know Mother Nature, the one who as the job of making sure our living planet Earth and all things that reside under Earth's roof are living and breathing. Mother nature does not regret the past or worry about the future, yet all tasks are accomplished with great skill in the present moment she lives in.

If you stop for a minute to analyze your life, all you really have that is yours and certain is the present moment. That present moment which happens to be right now! The sentence you are reading right now! Not the one before this sentence or the one after this sentence, but this sentence alone is the only true thing in your life. I know this may all seem a little deep at first, but bear with me, and I will try to make the point understood in plain English. You see the sentence you read before this one is gone; it is stored in your mind as memory. It may not appear as if that occurred, but believe me it did. Memories are instantaneous; the second that just passed is now a memory in your mind. Therefore, lets classify memories as the past because that is where memories reside. Once a memory, it is no longer a tangible piece of reality, it is gone. Now you can go right back up there and read that sentence again and at the exact present moment you are reading it, it is tangible. This tangible world is where I will attempt to take you. Confused? If you are not confused welcome; if you are confused let us continue deeper.

Past memories have a family member called future concerns. Future concerns are the sentence you are about to read. You do not know exactly what the sentence will read. All you can do is speculate on what the next sentence will read. The problem at hand is that the older we get and the more negative our frame of mind becomes, the speculating becomes a way of life. The speculation would be acceptable if it were positive, because that which we focus on we draw closer to. However, it is not positive, when negative frame of mind is involved, the speculation is negative, negative, and more negative. The only way to break this cycle is to understand that speculation and memories do not exist.

Neither past memories nor future concerns tangibly exists. You are not looking at it, you cannot touch it, smell it, hear it, nor taste it. It is not there, it merely stored in your mind as a memory or it is simply a non-existent speculation. The sentence here now is the only real thing you have. Put your finger on the sentence you are reading and stop for five seconds. That five seconds that just passed was all you should have been experiencing at that time. You should not have been thinking why am I doing this? Why did I eat that donut for breakfast? What am I going to do tomorrow? You should have only been focusing on your finger being on that sentence for five seconds, because that five seconds was the only tangible reality you had and it should not have been wasted on cluttering thoughts of the past or worrying thoughts of the future.

In our life, there are three places we can spend our conscious and sub-conscious lives, past, present, and future. For some odd reason as if we were programmed, the mass majority decides to live in the past, future, or both. The irony of it all is that there are three choices of where to live, and the only one that is real is very rarely chosen, the present.

To harbor a positive frame of mind, you will need to focus entirely in the present moment. The here and now is all you have, and if you utilize it effectively with a positive frame of mind your opportunity for total prosperity and greatness abound will be plentiful. You see, the world of past regret and future worry harbor negative thoughts and a negative frame of mind. They drain your conscious and sub-conscious energy of positive that exist inside you. When this negative takeover is accomplished, you might as well be a walking corpse. Instead of experiencing nothing real, tangible, and great that life has to offer, you merely feel nostalgia, regret, guilt, worry, anxiety, and speculation.

On the contrast, the world of the present can have no past regret and no future worry. For at this very second there is no regret, nor any worry. It is simply just you reading this book, nothing more nothing less; nothing bad, nor nothing good; nothing right, nor nothing wrong.

The present moment is the land of the real. When you live in the moment, your life begins to take on a newfound peace. You begin to realize all that you regret is gone and does not exist; you are where you are now because it is where you put yourself. If you want to change it simply change it one second at a time with no burden of past regret. You will see that the future is nothing but a mirage of water in a desert, an optical illusion if you will. It does not exist; the future is a blank slate neither bad nor good. The future will be what you make of it every second of your life. Energy does not need to be wasted on what you speculate of imaginary events. Understand, that there is no yesterday or tomorrow, there is only now.

Now is where you need to live to maintain a healthy positive frame of mind. Living in the moment is the foundation of total prosperity. Remember to live your life from this second forward, one-second at a time and I promise you a positive life and a positive frame of mind will follow.

YOU ATTRACT WHAT YOU GIVE

Individuals who posses a positive frame of mind have a firm grasp of the law of give and attract. The law is simply and extremely effective yet profoundly under used and often completely ignored by most of the world. The simply truth is everything you give in life you will get in return. The old saying you reap what you sow always holds true. The law of gives and attract is that simple. If you give off good karma, you will get good karma. If you give smiles, you will get smiles. If you give bad karma, you will get bad karma. If you give frowns, you will get frowns. Do you want people to treat you with respect and admiration? If so, you must live your life treating everyone around you in the manner in which you want others to treat you. If you want people to be more positive when they associate with you, become more positive when you associate with them. If you want others to stop treating you in a negative manner, stop treating yourself in a negative manner.

If you live a life in a negative frame of mind, you will in turn receive a life of negative. When you are walking around in that negative state of mind, it is there for the entire world to see and feel. Many people believe that this negative aura around them is only a part of their world and the world around them is not included in their own miseries. This is false. Everyone who is in contact with you is affected by this negative frame of mind. Your wife, husband, children, parents, grandparents, friends, peers, co-workers, girlfriends, boyfriends, pets, and anything else that's alive in your world is subjected to this negative world you choose to live in. In some form or another, they will be subjected to this negative frame of mind. If you constantly worry, your spouse is sure to feel the affects from your despondency. Your parents will feel sorrow for your worries. This will create a negative feeling from them when they think of you. Your children will sense the tension and begin to feel their own tension caused by your worries. When this negative tension is dispersed, it creates a negative tension in others. This negative tension will cause others to give you negative tension right back and the cycle will never end, it will only grow stronger and stronger feeding of each individuals negative frame of mind caused by one. The cycle can and must be broken and you must be the one to break it. Once you decide to change what you give, people around you will change in the manner in which they give to you. Have you ever noticed when you are watching a movie if someone is laughing you have a tendency to want to laugh or if someone is crying you have a tendency to want to cry. The same holds true in reality. If you treat someone with anger, you are sure to get anger in return. Just as a good sales person will attempt to kill an angry customer with kindness. That is because it is very hard to continue treating someone badly when they are treating you overly kind. The law of give and attract can be a very powerful tool in someone's life. If used properly and positively it can be a great enabling tool in your life and if used negatively it can be a great disabling tool in your life.

The great thing about this law is that it the rules are the same for a positive frame of mind. If you live a life with a positive frame of mind, you will create a life of positive for all those around you. The individual who posses a positive frame of mind can sit down at the end of the day, no matter how horrible it was, and still remain positive. When those around you that care or that are merely associated with you see that you are unbreakable and can remain positive and constant weathering whatever storm life blows your way, they will become drawn to your strength and positive frame of mind. This positive aura given of by *you* will in turn create a positive aura in the people around you. These individuals will enjoy the time spent with you drawing energy from your positive frame of mind. This will create an endless positive cycle where every time you are in contact with people they are treating you in a positive manner and you are treating them in a positive manner. When you use the law of give and attract with a positive frame of mind, you will create your own personal positive world, a world where you draw energy from others positive behavior towards you and they gain energy from your positive behavior towards them.

I think the point is clear. If you give off positive feelings to others, you will get positive feelings in return. If you give off negative feelings to others, you will receive negative feelings in return. Be sure to choose wisely, no matter if you choose to have a positive frame of mind or a negative frame of mind, it will be all around you. It will exist and penetrate every facet of your life. With a clear understanding of the impact the law of give and attract can have on your life, it should be imperative that you keep your frame of mind as positive as you possible can through good and bad times. Realize that when you are feeling lowly you will cause others to experience the negative aura and if you cannot change for yourself than do it for the ones you care about. I know you do not want your kids to grow up in a negative world, nor you spouse, nor any other loved ones. Keep yourself in a positive frame of mind and the world you are afraid of will disappear. The world you desire will then draw near.

PERCEPTION IS REALITY

A positive frame of mind runs in sequence with a positive perception of reality. By perception, I mean the way in which you view your life. Do you think you have a good life? Do you think you are fortunate? Do you think you had a good childhood? Are you thankful for the things that you currently have in your life? Do you feel life has many opportunities in store for you? Do you feel you are capable of accomplishing any goal you set in life? Do you have a positive self-image when you walk out the door in the morning to face the world? Your answers to these questions, will give you a good estimate of the quality of your perception of life. If your answers consist of yes to most of them then you probably already posses a positive frame of mind and a positive perception of reality. If your answers consist of no, kind of, or sometimes then it is time to do some reprogramming on your frame of mind to gain positive levels of perception.

If there is an individual in this world whom you are filled with envy because you think he/she has the perfect life, you may want to rethink your position. You see, just because you perceive this individuals life, as being perfectly rosy does not mean that the individual who is actually living the life you envy perceives their life as you do. The point is the life you envy in others does not exist because your perceptions will never be the same. The individual who actually lives the so called perfect life experiences the same human problems we do, they are not immune to human emotions that cause distress in our bodies such as, anger, quilt, regret, fear, hurt, envy, tension, and worry. These people wake up and put their clothes on just as we do in the morning and I am positive this *envied individual is not envying his own life.*

Now if you have ever truly met someone who was envious of there own life then that would be something to be envious of. I think that should be our goal, to become envious of our own lives through positive perception. To obtain this goal you will be faced with another life altering choice. You can choose to have a negative perception of your past, present, and future life, or you can choose to have a positive perception of your past, present, and future life.

An individual with a negative perception of their past, present, and future life will create a world of constant misery. People living with negative perception are never able to overcome there past childhood traumas, maybe they had an alcoholic parent, a loss of a sibling or parent, a divorce, trouble with the law, lived in poverty, or frequently moved from one town to another. Whatever their reason, they become so fixated on a negative perception of their lives that they are never able to see anything that comes to them as a positive. They begin to live a life of self-pity, which in turn creates failure mechanisms. These failure mechanisms caused by a negative life perception creates built in sub-conscious excuses such as, "If I screw my life up, I can always blame it on my parents, or all the bad things I have seen growing up." Failure mechanisms will follow these individuals their entire life. Instead of letting go and conquering the past problems to be more aware of positive present day opportunity, they carry their negative perceptions with them everywhere the go. This negative perception not only creates negative memories of the past, but creates negative memories in the present day as well. There is no possible way that an individual who has a negative perception of their past and present can have a positive perception of their future. This being so, there can be no chance of happiness and success. Once again, this will enter these individuals upon another negative cycle where past, present, and future constantly revolve around a negative perception.

Individuals who posses a positive perception of their life have an entirely different view than those of their negative perceiving counterparts. Regardless of how good or bad these individuals life may have been, they see there live as being positive. An individual who perceives his/her life as positive will see their life as being fun, challenging, enjoyable, adventurous, exciting, and full of love. These individuals walk through life with a positive frame of mind ready to conquer any challenge. They answer yes to the questions listed in the first paragraph. These individuals can go through life free of the heavy emotional burdens of guilt, regret, sorrow, fear, worry, and low self-worth. A positive perception is a powerful tool against the hardships of daily life. Positive perception can bring energy and strength in times where others will crumble. It will give you a sense of faith that everything will turn out for the best, because if you are positive about everything up until this point then you are bound to be positive for the rest of your life. Looking at everything in a positive perception, *bad or good* will create an unbreakable positive frame of mind. The reason I say *bad or good*, is that every occurrence in your life can be looked upon as a positive experience or a negative experience. For example, if you dealt with alcoholism growing up, you can view this as a life altering negative experience that destroys your spirit, you can blame it on yourself, and you can live the rest of your life with no self-esteem, or you can view this as a character builder that taught you how to deal with adversity and real life problems, you can view this as a test from above to see how well you can overcome adversity, you can view this as something that has made you into a resilient, extraordinary human being, and you can have the understanding that your family members alcoholism is not your fault and vow to only let it destroy one life instead of two. You see, for every bad, there is a good. You can view negative events as negative events and positive events as negative events or you can choose negative events as positive events and positive events as positive events. The choice of how to view any experience of your life is entirely up to you. It is never to late to look back on your life and change an experience that you have previously been viewing as a negative perception to a positive perception.

Many people believe individuals who walk around perceiving everything positive are simply blessed or have excellent personality traits, as if these individuals posses something abnormal that the average person can never posses. That way of thinking is total incorrect if you do not already posses a positive perception you can learn to have a positive perception. You can take two people who have lived almost identical lives or siblings for that matter who have grown up in the exact same household, and if on of them has a negative perception of their life upbringing and the other one has a positive perception of their upbringing, one life story will be greatly conflicting with the other. The degree of success and prosperity the positive and negative perceivers have will differ greatly as well. With this being so, it is not the type of life that you have lived that has caused your negative perception, instead it is the way you are perceiving your life experiences that has caused a negative perception. Therefore, it is not the experience itself, but rather how you perceive the experience. How you perceive your life experiences is entirely up to you. Here again, the majority appears to elect in choosing to perceive most of their life experiences as negative ones. Almost as if they want to walk around with this negative burden their entire lives. The reason I feel you can learn positive perception is you have the decision to choose how you view a particular incident in your life. Anytime you have the ability to make a choice, correcting the matter is merely *learning* to choose the right decision, which in this case it would be learning to choose the positive view instead of the negative view. At the exact point in time, you begin to view a particular incident in your life as a positive experience instead of a negative experience you will begin to feel changes within yourself. It is as if you can feel your frame of mind growing increasingly positive. Just because you have perceived an event in your life as negative for years, does not mean you cannot change your perception of that experience right know. It is never too late to change your perception of life events.

The importance of changing your life perceptions is far more beneficial than you can ever imagine. With this being so, it is not the type of life that you have lived that has caused your negative perception, instead it is the way you are perceiving your life experiences that has caused a negative perception. It is entirely up to you the type of life perception you choose. You can choose to have a negative perception or a positive perception. Choosing a positive perception allows your mind to be free of negative burden, your frame of mind will then have a notion to stay fixated on the positive constantly expecting something positive to be just around the corner, and expecting something positive will general yield positive which in turn creates a positive cycle of past, present, and future. Your perception is your reality and your perception is your choice. If you desire a true positive frame of mind, it is time for you to make a change and begin to train your mind to perceive everything in a positive way.

RECOGNIZING PERSONAL PROBLEMS

The only way to ever posses a positive frame of mind that is free from negative emotions is to solve all your personal problems. Personal problems are exactly that, problems that are very personal to you individually. Every individual's personal problems are different from the next and the degree of impact the problem has on that individual's life will differ as well. There are people who can have a pet die on them, grieve for a few hours and then go out and buy a new. On the other hand, there are people who can have a pet die and they need therapy for the next five years. The individual who can get over his/her pet passing may not be able to handle other problems quite as well as the individual who grieves severely for their pet. The point is we are all very different individuals and a personal problem is a personal problem. Keeping this in mind, we should all be very understanding of others problems regardless if you think they are severe or not. You never know how severe the actual individual who is experiencing the problem perceives the problem. For example, there are young teenagers today who commit suicide or murder because someone at school is making fun of the clothes they where. To an adult, our problems seem far superior to a kid catching jokes thrown at them for wearing bad clothes. Our problems are *real*. The truth is, at that point in time these young individuals perceive their problems as great as ours if not greater. In many cases, these problems will be brushed aside as meaningless. Not properly recognizing the problem will in turn create disaster.

Everyone's personal problems need to be addressed and solved. When you can recognize, sympathize, and solve personal problems in others, it will create a more positive frame of mind in yourself and the individual you are helping. Many our current national tragedies may have never occurred if the parents only spent time with their children trying to create solutions to their personal problems. Sometimes helpful and encouraging advice is all one needs, and in many cases professional advice is in order, but it is imperative whatever the personal problem, that it be addressed and solved.

Only when you can learn to recognize, sympathize, and solve problems in others, will you be able to recognize, sympathize, and solve personal problems within yourself. Many of the parents who have had their children take their own life or the life of another have not only ignored the problem in their child, they have also been ignoring their own personal problems for a number of years.

The only way to solve personal problems within yourself and others is to bring it to the surface and talk about it objectively. If you have problems with your childhood, you need to talk the pain out with someone you care about or someone you respect and feel you can confide in. If there is no one in your life that fits that description, you then I suggest talking to a professional about it. When you can bring your problems to the surface, you stand a much greater chance of understanding the root of the problem. When you find the root of the problem, you can begin to gain a better understanding of why it is making you feel a certain way. The worst thing that can happen is to let a personal problem go ignored and never understanding why it is crippling other areas of your personal life. You see personal problems are a disease on the soul. They do not only affect one aspect of your life, instead they bleed into all aspects of your life, affecting your happiness, health, finances, and frame of mind. For example, if someone was mentally or physically abused as a child, they may choose to block it out in their sub-conscious and try to forget that it happened for the rest of their life. Meanwhile they are finding themselves in a constant negative frame of mind, never successful, never happy, and often times abusive to the ones that care about them like their own children. These people are doing nothing more than living out a constant cycle of a negative unhappy life. Their parents abused them, they will abuse their kids, and so on and so on, until someone is smart enough to break the cycle by recognizing there is a problem and learning to cure the problem.

Once a problem is recognized and brought to the surface, there is no place for it to hide. It is out of your sub-conscious mind and back in your conscious mind, where it can no longer secretly destroy your life. The moment you recognize your problem you can then begin to analyze why you are pre-disposed to act a particular way. The abused victim may then find themselves being abusive to others and step back for a minute to say, "wait a minute, I am just behaving this way because it is only natural for me to, it is all I have ever known and I am taking my anger out on others that are innocent and do not need to be subjected to this kind of treatment." When the cause and effects of the problem are understood they can then be broken and solved.

When you begin to understand one personal problem you will then begin to understand all your personal problems and what negative effects they are having on your life. At this point of recognition, the personal problems can then be cured. In many cases, it is merely as simple as recognizing the problem and bringing to the surface. Once it is at the surface of your mind, your mind alone can find a way to cure the problem.

To have a positive frame of mind, no personal problem can go ignored in yourself and the loved ones around you. No matter the size of your problem, if it is causing you negative emotions or it is causing you to live in a negative frame of mind, it must be addressed. A personal problem can consist of many things; it can be someone you are anger with, you job, the car you drive, where you live, how you look, how your spouse looks, how you behave, how your kids behave, how your spouse behaves, the type of childhood you lived, where you went to school, where you did not go to school, the things you have done, the things you should have done, the things you think you are going to do, the things you think your spouse or kids are going to do, how you sleep at night, the clothes you wear, the negative way you think, the negative way your spouse and kids think, the way your spouse is raising your kids; personal problems are everywhere, it is just a matter if they are a problem for you or the ones you love. If you live in a negative frame of mind, just make a list of possible personal problems in your life and ask yourself if it is a problem, your soul will give you a true answer. If personal problems exist, they need to be recognized and a curing process needs to begin. Only then, will you and your loved ones be able to live a life free of negative emotions and negative behavior, fully possessing a positive frame of mind no matter what the situation.

DEDICATION

An individual who posses a positive frame of mind will also posses a strong dedication value in life. Dedication for greatness, happiness, and everything the positive heart desires. When an individual is dedicated to a cause they become focused on that cause. Your first dedication should be that you allow yourself to be happy and control a positive frame of mind while you are alive. To be dedicated to such a cause does not mean that you casually try to work at your happiness and frame of mind when you feel the time is right or when you happen to be thinking about. To be dedicated to such a cause means that you devote every waking second of your life to becoming happy, possessing a positive frame of mind at all times no matter how challenging the test. Dedication involves constantly working and thriving to improve your mental quality of life.

When you become dedicated to possessing a positive frame of mind your mind will not allow you to drift into the negative behavior that you are accustom to. Dedicating yourself to a cause allows your mind to give 110 percent of its efforts to remain on the cause you are dedicating yourself to. When you are not dedicated, you simply let your mind choose whatever cause happens to be fitting at that particular moment in time. This will usually be based completely on how you are feeling emotionally throughout each day. For example, if you allow yourself to become upset from a bad day of work, your mind will begin to focus on how upset you are and become dedicate to your upsetting emotions at that particular time. Your mind will then continue to stay focused and dedicated to that particular emotion until you begin to focus on another emotion. In this case, negative emotions will lead you to focus on other negative emotions in which your mind is constantly dedicated to negative thoughts. At this point, you will have imprisoned your mind to dedicate itself to posses a continuous negative frame of mind.

To break the negative pattern, you must dedicate and train yourself to stay focused on nothing but positive thoughts. Instead of letting yourself experience anger caused by external forces, such as a bad day at the office, understand that the moment you allow the anger to enter your mind you are allowing yourself to become dedicated to a negative frame of mind, a frame of mind that will rob and blind you from your daily happiness and success. The moment you understand that allowing negative thoughts to enter your mind will cause a temporary dedication to negative behavior, you will begin to block out any negative feelings that try to penetrate your mind. Awareness of the power a negative thought has over your mind will allow you to build a strong defense against the negative thoughts that will try to invade your happiness.

When you arrive at the awareness of negative dedication you can then become dedicated to injecting positive thoughts into your mind 24 hours a day. The more dedicated you become to keeping positive thoughts flowing, the more likely you will become to possessing a positive frame of mind. Believe me, you can never have enough positive thoughts entering your mind. There is no such thing as someone who is too positive, too happy, or too successful. When you experience the possession of a positive frame of mind, it will become addictive. You will never want to go back to your old way of thinking again.

When you have fully dedicated yourself to possessing a positive frame of mind, other areas of your life will become more positive as well. You will not only be changing your life for the better, you will be changing the quality of life of all the people that live in your world for the better. You will become dedicated to all things that are positive, like maintaining healthy relationships, job success, proper parenting, giving, becoming a better role model, spirituality, kindness, compassion, and love. Dedication to the positive will enrich your life in more ways than can ever be described.

Life is short, and now is the time to stop letting your mind choose your dedications based on your daily emotions caused by external forces. It is time to make the choice internally to dedicate yourself to possessing a positive frame of mind 24 hours a day 7 days a week. Choose a positive dedication that is based on sound principles of happiness, a dedication that ignores your own negative daily emotions caused by external forces. When you dedicate yourself to a positive frame of mind, there will be no turning back, you will be moving forward into a better direction. Into a direction that leads you to a place of true happiness, where total prosperity can and will exist.

SEARCH FOR INSPIRATION

A good way to maintain a healthy, positive frame of mind is to search for inspiration. Inspiration can be people; places, stories, movies, music, and anything else that makes you feel positive inside. I recommend searching for inspiration everywhere you are, everyday you can. It could be the single mother of three who's third job is at your local restaurant; the children who are fighting cancer at the local pediatric hospital; successful people who have overcome a childhood in housing projects; recovered addicts; and love stories. Inspirational stories are everywhere if you open your eyes, even in your mirror. Searching for inspiration will allow your mind to continue on, in a positive mind frame.

Many times on your quest for inspiration, it can lead you into other positive avenues where you can see, learn, and feel new things in life. You may learn new and interesting things about people and places that you never thought were possible. If there is someone that you admire, try to find out more about who they are. Try to learn what they have done to get them to where they are in life. If there is a story that inspires you of someone who overcame great adversity to achieve their goals such as Lance Armstrong, try to find out what motivated them to survive and conquer their adversity. Learn what they think to succeed. When you begin to learn the traits of successful people, you can learn to incorporate them in your own life as well. You may learn new and interesting things about the different stories successful people have on their road to success. Many stories may really surprise you as to how rocky the road to success can sometimes be. Reading inspirational stories and books will also keep your mind focused on the positive. Each inspirational book or story you come across, take the time to read it and learn the message each as to offer. If there are movies or music that inspire you, try to watch or listen to them as much as possible to help you stay inspired daily. Find an inspirational place that gives you energy and peace. Maybe it is a post card or maybe it is in your backyard. Regardless, spend time there even if you can only imagine you are there. Take a few minutes each day and visit this place for inspiration and peace of mind.

Searching for inspiration is a simple daily tool that can bring great happiness and peace of mind to your life. You will begin to realize that even great successful people everywhere and they are no different than you or I. They deal with adversity and problems just as we do, and they have overcome them just as we will. Finding inspiration will allow you will take on an

97

understanding that you too can accomplish anything and overcome anything any life if you put your mind to it and focus positively. I have a friend who came from nothing and is very successful, he told me one time that he wakes up an hour earlier than normal every morning and reads inspirational books until he fills charged up enough to take on the day with a positive frame of mind. He said sometimes it takes five minutes and he said sometimes it takes the full hour, but he said it always charges his positive frame of mind. I have begun trying it and it really works. If you want a daily positive charge, try it.

AVOIDING THE MEDIA

Abstaining from the media is an excellent way to avoid negative emotions. The media always has an angle to every story, the majority of the time that angle is to make the common public worry about their safety, or war, or economic crash, or racism, or weather disasters, or all the violence that will be coming to your town in the near future. The media seems to be the epitome of all mankind's negative emotions; the emotions that keep the majority of us living in an unhappy world; emotions such as anger, fear, guilt, greed, lust, envy, regret, anxiety, uncertainty, and doubting your faith. As if it is not enough that these emotions have been instilled in us since childbirth as being normal; you now get to sit in front of your television or newspaper and get a 30 minute daily overdose of these negative, worthless emotions only to make sure you do not have a chance of thinking positive and trusting yourself and the world you live in.

What you here and read about from the media is what you will need to avoid if you want to reach total prosperity. Believe me, you will be able to keep up with current events through the power of osmosis. There are plenty of people out there who are addicted to the media, and they enjoy spreading the bad news. If you feel you cannot go cold turkey then I recommend you cut your daily dosage in half. If you watch 30 minutes a day try watching 15 minutes a day. If you find yourself feeling better, which you probably will, try to cut it down to 10 minutes and day. Eventually you will realize that you do not need the media as much as they need you. The media preys on the weak, they want to show them controversy, violence, and scandal, as if the more fear and doubt they create in the public the better story they have told. I guess it could be called negative sensationalism. For every negative story, they could at least give us one positive story to offset the negative story. I guess that is just too much to ask.

I am not telling you how to live your life by saying, "try to watch half as less news everyday as you normally do," I am merely making a suggestion to something I know has made my life a much more positive. I can tell you if you are thriving for a positive frame of mind, the media is a tool that will try to detour you from that. I no it does not sound good to tell you that your own media is pumping you full of negative emotions, but is nothing more than factual. I do not understand why they continue on this negative course nor do I know if it will ever stop. Who knows, maybe the reason behind the media's negative emotional overdose, is our governments does not want the entire world walking around in a positive frame of mind; a frame of mind that allows an individual to not be afraid to leave a miserable job and search for a better life, merely on the notion that they know and feel there is something better out there waiting on. When you are constantly experiencing negative emotions, you are constantly in a state of fear, self-doubt, and worry. This state of mind is where we are most controllable, docile, and passive. This is the state of mind where people will continue living their days in a routine regardless of their happiness, simply because they do not know what their identity will be without their unhappy routine. I am sure there are thousands of theories as to why the media overdoses us with negative emotions, maybe we will never know, the only thing we can do is realize that they do overdose us with negative emotions and try to listen with a hollow ear. I have one peace of mind, and that is I do know that I can choose what to watch, read, and listen to and what not to watch, read, and listen, and so can you!

Could you imagine if ever time you came home after a long day of work to sit down to some news on the television, and there be nothing but positive motivational stories on, and positive teachers letting the public know that it is okay to think and be positive and happy. You would probably get up and do something positive the rest of the night feeling great all the while. We know it is not a perfect world and that will never happen. What can happen is that you choose what goes in your mind; do you want to watch, read, or listen to something that is attempting to fill your mind with negative emotions or do you want to watch, read, or listen to something that is going to attempt to fill your mind with positive emotions. If you thrive for a constant positive frame of mind, I recommend you favor the positive stories and avoid the media.

QUESTION EVERYTHING

Individuals who have a positive frame of mind question everything negative in life, be it the media, people, work, society, and any daily negative life experience. If for some rare reason they are listening to the media, unlike the common public, they do not believe everything the media tells them. They understand that the media has angles to everything and they have the ability to read in between the lines. If it is someone treating them negatively they do not accept it as if they deserve it, they ask why and search for the correct answer. If there job is causing negative emotions, instead of taking it home with them and feeling poorly, they ask why; what they can do about it; and how they are going to go about correcting the problem? Questioning negative things involves ask questions such as, what? Where? Why? How? When? And Who? Questioning everything negative gives your mind ammunition to fight off any negative emotion that attempts to infiltrate your life.

Questioning all negative emotions allows you to take from things what you want to feel and choose the things you do not want to feel. If something negative occurs in your life, instead of just accepting it and accepting the feelings that follow, ask yourself why and search for the positive door that the negative occurrence is leading you to. Anytime a window of opportunity is closed in our life, another exciting opportunity is opening. Many people cannot see the new positive opportunity because they are still feeling poorly about the negative one that has just closed. They are not questioning why this occurred, and where is it leading me? Without question, they are simply stuck accepting their own created negative, unquestioned, unchallenged, misery.

Anytime a negative occurrence happens in your life large or small, question it. When you begin to ask why, how, what, who, where, you may begin to see this negative occurrence in its true form, opportunity. You should never accept any negative in your life without question. When you accept a negative emotion, you are telling yourself that it is okay for this feeling to be in my mind. You will be inviting a negative emotion into your life, and one negative emotion will invite all its friends, and believe me, they have many friends.

When questioning these negative emotions caused by numerous external sources, you should ask yourself if there is validity to this negative emotion? Do you want this negative emotion in your mind? Is this negative emotion healthy? How will this negative emotion make you feel? What is this negative emotion going to do for me? The answers to the questions above should be no, no, no, bad, and nothing. After the questioning, your mind will begin to recognize any negative emotion as not welcome, and unhealthy. You will then become trained to feel only positive emotions and your mind will let no negative emotion pass without questioning and interrogation.

CONCLUSION

I hope this series of thoughts and principles will add some enlightenment and understanding in your life as to what it means to have a positive frame of mind. Once an understanding is developed, the principles in this chapter can be used as ammunition and defense against all negative that invades your life. Just as a martial artist uses sound principles to defend against attackers of their peace, you will have sound principles to defend against negative emotional attackers of your frame of mind, and like anything in life, the more you practice the better you will get and the easier it will become. There is no substitute for a positive frame of mind; it is a rare and precious thing; the majority do not posses it; everyone desires it; it cannot be bought or sold; and when you posses a positive frame of mind, nothing or no one can take it away from you. When you walk out the door possessing a positive frame of mind, you will be one-step ahead in the search for happiness than the individuals who do not posses a positive frame of mind. You can then teach others of what it takes to have a positive frame of mind and what it means to live in true happiness. This newly found positive frame of mind is going to give you the ability to create your own destiny as you see fit. The things you want and desire in life, including total prosperity can all be yours if you pursue them with a positive frame of mind.

When you begin to make the change toward a positive frame of mind use all the thoughts and principles in this chapter. Maintain a conscious awareness of your frame of mind and how you are feeling. Feel that you deserve happiness and success in your life. Always remain internally controlled and never let the external world control your frame of mind. Never look back in regret and sorrow or look forward in doubt and worry, stay focused in the present moment; it's the only real experience you have at the moment and do not let your mind pass it by with pre-occupied thoughts of past and future. Keep the understanding that what you attract you will always get in return, and if you want something such as happiness, then give happiness. Remember your perception of the world you live is your reality, so make sure your perceptions are positive. Recognize all your personal problems and diligently search for a cure for these problems. Dedicate your life to becoming one of the rare individuals who posses a positive frame of mind. Search for inspiring words every day of your life. Avoid the media every chance you get, and question everything negative that exist in your world. If you follow these thoughts and principles daily, possessing a positive frame of mind will become inevitable. Never vary from these thoughts and remain focused on your goal. If you make a devotion to yourself to make these thoughts and principles of a positive frame of mind second nature in your life, you will begin to understand what it truly means to live in happiness and you will then be on a clear path to total prosperity!

Life will only be as good as you decide it will be!!

CHAPTER 5

RELATIONSHIPS

RELATIONSHIPS OCCUPY A VAST MAJORITY of our lives. Relationships consist of our daily interactions with our selves, friends, peers, co-workers, bosses, spouses, significant others, loved ones, and anyone else you have daily contact with. The statuses of these relationships play an important role in your overall happiness and frame of mind. If you tend to have good relationships with all those you are exposed to, then you are more than likely a very positive, happy, successful individual. Individuals who are happy and positive internally have a tendency to portray that happiness in their relationships. If you tend to have good relations with some, but not others, then you probably have a tendency to be happy at times and frustrated at times. These individuals may have a good relationship with their spouse, but maintain a bad relationship with others, such as, their boss, friends, and co-workers. This may leave them feeling happy at home, but miserable when they leave the presence of the one they are comfortable with. If you have a tendency to have conflict with all those you encounter, then you are probably living a frustrated, negative, confused life. These individuals tend to be negative in nature and negative with all those they are in contact with. They are more than likely unhappy within themselves and tend to portray their unhappiness in their external relationships. You see our relations with others are a direct reflection of our own happiness. It is hard to give happiness to your relationships when you are unhappy inside, and when you are happy inside; it is much easier to give happiness to your relationships. You will never have a balanced, happy existence if your relationships without having happiness in yourself.

Your relationships are a vital factor to your overall total prosperity. How can you achieve total prosperity if your relationships are not very prosperous? You must learn to improve your relationships in order to have a balanced prosperous life. When learning is involved, the first thing you must do is gain understanding and knowledge. An understanding and knowledge of what it takes to have prosperous and healthy relationships with all. Once again, there are simple solutions involved to improving your relationships, if you comprehend and practice these solutions your relationships will improve and your overall quality of life will improve. Solutions to improving your relationships include: Understanding your most basic relationship, which is the one personal relationship you have with yourself; Understanding the nature of others; communication; confidence and trust; patience; listening; pride; losing the fear of showing emotions; respect; body language; avoidance; and visualizing the type of relationships you desire. When you understand and implement these solutions into your life, you will then be able to maximize the potential of relationship you have and wish to have.

All individuals thrive for better relationships; it is just that many do not know how to go about improving them. If you are one of these individuals who desire to improve relationships, but never had any true understanding of what it took to accomplish such a feat, now is the time to implement these solutions into your life, so you can look forward to a better tomorrow. These relationship improvement solutions are a very beneficial tool for incorporating overall happiness in your life. Any individual who does not have excellent relationships and excellent relationship skills will never be able to experience total prosperity in their lives. If you desire happiness, success, fulfillment and overall total prosperity, it will be mandatory that you understand and incorporate these solutions into your life. As with any positive solution, they all work well in accordance with the other. When you begin to implement one relationship solution into your life, the next solution will be that much easier to understand and implement. Since there are quite a few relationship solutions, I recommend you begin implementing one relationship solution at a time into your life. You can start from the top and work your way down, or you can pick the solutions you feel you need most improving on and master them first. After you have understood and implemented each relationship solution into your life, you should then be able to notice a substantial positive change in yourself and those around you.

PERSONAL RELATIONSHIP

Your personal relationship is the relationship you have with yourself. This relationship is the foundation of all relationships. If you have a good relationship with yourself and you have a friendship with yourself, then you more than likely have a good relationship with others around you and attract many friendships. If you have a negative under developed relationship, unrecognizing and ignoring your inner voice, then you probably have un-prosperous and unhealthy relationships with others around you and find yourself lacking in friendships and loving, meaningful relationships. The degree to which we can feel contentment and happiness with our own selves is the degree of happiness you will experience from other external relationships, and the degree to which we can develop a friendship and relationship within our selves, is the degree to which we can develop success, friendships, and healthy loving relationships in our lives. How can one have prosperous external relationships when their relationship with their own inner being is not in harmony?

A good inner relationship is your first step to possessing successful external relationships. The posses a healthy inner relationship with yourself, you must first understand what a healthy inner relationship consist of. The inner relationship we have with ourselves is the one that involves the inner voice inside of all of us. Only you hear this voice, because it resides in your own sub-conscious. This is the inner voice that says, "I can do it", or "I cannot do it." When you ignore this inner relationship, it may make your life decisions for you, when you listen and comprehend this inner relationship, you make your life decisions as you see fit. You see there may be challenges in your life that you have failed at before you even attempt them because you have a negative inner relationship. Without even noticing your inner voice, it may be telling you, "there is no way you can do this, you do not have what it takes", before you even walk out the door, leaving you no chance of life success and happiness. Many people go through their entire life unhappy and unsuccessful without every considering an undeveloped, total negative inner relationship as the primary source of their problem. A positive relationship with their inner being is never developed, leaving all their fear, self-doubt, and worry to make their life decisions for them. When all that would need to be done to develop a positive inner relationship would be to recognize and listen to this inner voice. Once you recognize and listen to this inner voice, you can begin to hear exactly what is going on inside yourself. Recognizing and listening to this inner voice gives you the opportunity to dispute the negative feedback your inner-self is giving you. Once a dispute is brought forth within your inner being of the negative feedback being displaced on your mind, an inner relationship is developed.

The majority of the people in this world never develop their inner relationship. If they only realized that once an inner relationship is developed, the negativity in their inner being can never control their life again. When an inner relationship is developed, listening and recognizing, your inner voice is involved. If you have a big job interview and your inner voice is saying, "I do not think I am going to get this job, I never do good in interviews, do not get your hopes up", if you have a developed inner relationship, you can listen to these inner remarks and reply with "I do not want to hear that, I can get this job and I will, I am an asset to any company, my interview success rate may not be high, but I am about to change that." Even if you have not reached a positive level within yourself and you do not totally believe the positive counter attacks on the negative responses, a dispute to the negative responses can be enough to change your views. When you begin to dispute these negative inner responses you will soon believe the positive disputes you are giving to the negative remarks. You see when an inner dispute has occurred the negative responses that once ruled your life without question are now being disputed. An internal dialogue has begun in which your negative responses have to give an explanation to there negative reactions. If your inner voice is saying, "I can not", and you recognize, listen, and dispute that with, "I can", then your inner relationship will begin to question by saying, "why do I always say I cannot;" "it is not as if I want to fail in life;"" If I want to get this job, I need to be saying I can;"" I cannot is not a response I want to focus on in this situation, so I am going to ignore this response." When this type of dialogue as occurred your inner voice begins to work together with you as a team. Your inner relationship begins to become one that is a friendship, where you become your own best friend constantly picking yourself up rising to the occasion in time of need.

When a true inner friendship is developed and you become your own best friend, there is no obstacle that cannot be overcome or any goal that cannot be obtained. An inner friendship will allow your inner responses to be in accordance with the outcome that is desired. When you become your own best friend, you will be taking a giant step towards making all your relationships prosperous. A friendship within you opens the door of opportunity and success. An inner friendship also increases prosperity in your life by making it much easier to make friends with others; by obtaining lasting loving relationships; by gaining respect and admiration from your peers, friends, co-workers, spouses, and bosses; by finding the career of your dreams; and by possessing relationship prosperity which will help guide you to the land of total prosperity. All these things are possible when a positive internal relationship is developed because your internal responses will be in accordance with the outcome you desire. Anytime your inner voice is giving the proper positive feedback to your desired outcome, the success rate of you obtaining that desired outcome is increased 100 percent as compared to your inner dialogue being undeveloped, unrecognized, and ignored, allowing your internal responses to fall out of accordance with your desired outcome. If you want to have prosperous healthy relationships with others, make it a point to develop the personal relationship within yourself. You can obtain lasting prosperous relationships in your life only when you can develop a strong relationship and friendship within yourself. When your inner voice says, "I can, I will," and gives you positive responses when you make mistakes like, "It's okay to make a mistake or fail every now and then, if I learn from it, I will only grow stronger, and I can turn this temporary failure into a lasting success as it strengthens my character." These types of responses are responses of a true inner friendship and when they occur in your life, you will be ready to develop successful prosperous external relationships with others.

THE NATURE OF OTHERS

A very helpful tool to developing successful external relationships with others involves understanding the nature of others. Understanding the nature of others involves an acquired skill of reading individuals personalities, understanding individual's likes and dislikes, and realizing the motivation of others. When you develop these attributes, you will acquire the ability to understand the nature of others. A successful positive relationship with another individual will depend greatly on your ability to understand that particular individual. The more you understand someone, the better your relationship will become. It is very difficult to have a prosperous relationship with someone without ever truly understanding that particular individual. It should be a goal to maximize your relationships by becoming someone who understands the nature of those individuals with whom a relationship is present, and with those who a relationship is desired. A good example would be the movie *Ground Hog Day*;

the character in the movie was a very shallow man who never really took the time to know the individuals around him where relationships were present. For that, deep down he was an unhappy man, lonely man inside. His fellow peers and co-workers never appeared to respect or like him for his shallow behavior. He was succumbed to a blessed curse in which he continually had to live the same day over and over, ground hog day. He had a crush on an attractive co-worker and each day he would try to get her home with him at night using lowly pick up lines that fit his shallow personality to a tee. After numerous strike-outs waking up empty handed and having to start the day over from scratch, his frustrations lead him to take a different approach, he began trying to understand the true nature of this individual. No longer was he interested in just taking her home for another hollow evening with someone of the opposite sex, he was truly interested in finding out what made her soul tick. For this, he began to truly understand her nature, by understanding her true nature, a special, healthy, prosperous relationship was developed and true love ensued shortly thereafter. Realizing how much he could learn and grow from understanding someone on a deeper level, he began to listen and understand all those around him with whom he had a relationship with, allowing him to develop a prosperous relationship with all individuals he came in contact with in the course of a single day. By understanding the true nature of others, this man was able to find true love, lasting friendships, and respect from his peers, and co-workers in the course of a single day. The moral being, the more you allow yourself to understand the true nature of others the more your relationships with others will develop into prosperous and positive relationships, and these positive relationships allow your inner being to grow more positive. When this occurs, your life exits the world of the superficial shallow and into a world of deep spiritual understanding and growth in yourself and your relationships with others.

Aiding in your understanding of the nature of others is the acquired ability to read individuals personalities. I say, "acquired ability", because this is an attribute you are not born with. You learn this attribute from many years of meeting many different individuals and having relationships with many different individuals. I acquired my ability to read people through my years of experience and travel. Growing up I moved quite a bit and lived in many different places. Throughout my experience I began to notice something rather peculiar about individuals I was meeting at a fairly earlier age. The peculiar thing I began to pick up on was that I could be in a town in an entirely different state and meet an individual who's personality, and often time looks and mannerisms, reminded me very much of someone I had already met hundreds of miles away. This finding fascinated me, so I began to experiment with it. I began to treat the indidviduals whom I had just met exactly like I treated the individuals whom I had already known in another town. Having a positive relationship with the former individual I had already known, I felt confident I would develop a positive relationship with this individual. My experiment actually worked, the individuals whom reminded me of one another had almost identical responses to occurrences. It was almost as if it were the same person. Taking what I had learned from my experiment made it very easy for me to make new friends and adapt to new situations very easily. What I had learned was the ability to read people. The more I became attuned to this newly acquired attribute the more I realized that these similar personality types are everywhere, they may even be living next door to one another. You do not have to move around your whole life to acquire the ability read people, although it is helpful, you simply need to keep yourself observant of individuals around you. When you become observant of individuals, you will begin to realize the personality similarities of individuals. Through my experiment I came to hypothesize that there are only so many personality types out there and we all fit somewhere into the mold of one. This is where the ability to read people comes into play. When you acquire the ability to read people, you will be able to determine an individual's personality shortly after meeting them, sometimes in minutes. The bonus of determining the personality type allows you to have a pre-determination of how this person is going to react to certain situations. If you are not one of a worldly nature and have never been in encountered by many different personalities, upon meeting individuals simply keep yourself observant and see if you notice any similarities with anyone, a movie star for example. If you meet someone that reminds you of a movie star, read them as if you would imagine the movie star they remind you of behaving to certain situations. Now no one is perfect and I have been wrong on one or two of my reads in my day and I am sure you will to, but the more you practice reading individuals the more you will begin to understand them. By reading individuals you are simply trying to acquire a pre-understanding of their nature, so you can develop a positive, prosperous relationship.

Understanding individual's likes and dislikes is very similar to reading someone's personality. For once, you feel confident in a personality read, you should already have a good understanding of that particular individuals likes and dislikes. If you do not feel confident in your particular read of an individual and you feel it will take time, then make it a point to first learn their likes and dislikes. When you understand someone's likes and dislikes, it is much easier to carry on a prosperous relationship with that individual. For example, I was never able to read my wife's personality initially. In the beginning of our relationship, we would have arguments from time to time because we did not understand what we liked to hear and what we did not like to hear. When you get to know someone long enough, you acquire the ability to read his or her personality type through attrition, as I did with my wife. Through time, I finally understood my wife's likes and dislikes and I knew what to say and what not to stay if I wanted peace or if I wanted war. Understanding likes and dislikes is not just for your spouse or significant other, it is for everyone you have a relationship and plan to have a relationship with. For example, if you know your boss likes golf, try to keep your conversations about golf or any other likes as long as you can before it turn to business. When you can center yourself on individuals likes, you stand a much greater chance for a prosperous relationship with that individual. They will enjoy being around you because the conversation is centered on something they like. If you do not fully know a particular individual's likes and dislikes that share a relationships with you, then I suggest you begin a diligent search for them, starting with the relationship that is most important to you. As soon as you understand the likes and dislikes of in your individual relationships, you will begin to see them grow much healthier and prosperous.

An important factor in gaining a better understanding of nature of others, is to understand and realize others motivations. The motivations of others can be considered their driving forces in life. The things that make them get up in the morning and take on the challenges of life. Taking the time to understand the individual's motivations that share relationships with you will enable you and your relationships to grow and prosper by gaining a better understanding of the relationship you share with that individual and how to maximize the potential happiness and prosperity of the relationship with that individual, and by learning to not be selfish with your time by giving your time to supporting and helping others. Keep in mind; realizing individuals' motivators will not come over night. However, if you remain attentive in these relationships and keep focused on searching for the motivations of others, they will become apparent. When you begin to understand individual's motivations, you will begin to understand that there are two motivations in life, positive motivations, and negative motivations, and you can then begin to offer support for their positive motivations, and help in restructuring their negative motivations. The point where you and your relationships begin to grow and become prosperous is the point when you can offer extra positive support and confidence to the positive motivations of the individuals who share relationships with you, and offer help and restructuring to the individuals who maintain negative motivations in their life. Offering positive support by fully understanding their motivations and respecting how they feel about them, not by offering your opinion of what you think of their motivations and what you think their motivations need to be, and offering help and restructuring to negative motivators by caring and using positive restructuring, not by offering opinionated negative criticism and righteous lectures. For example, if you know someone whose motivation is for happiness, success, a good job, and exercising. Then you should support this positive motivation. If you happen to find this individual feeling depressed or lousy, give them a call to pep them up, tell them they should start back exercising so they will feel better. If you know someone whose motivation is a dozen jelly donuts in the morning and a twelve pack of beer in the evening, then you should help this individual in restructuring their negative motivators in a caring and supportive manner by suggesting positive cures to their negative motivators. Perhaps suggest they find healthier eating habits or begin an exercise program for the sake of their health. If you stay in shape maybe you could offer for them to begin working out with you, or if you are out of shape maybe you could help them and help yourself by asking them to start getting in shape with you. The point is, as long as you are supportive and helpful in the motivations of others, you will be giving your time and positive energy to a cause of another and that is something extremely positive that others will gain strength from; and this positive giving is sure to be reciprocated back to you. Just think of how you feel or would feel about someone who gives their time and support to the motivations of others without any thought of themselves. I am sure you would think highly of this individual, and if there is someone you know who fits that description I am sure you see them as someone very special. When you begin to understand the motivation of others, you will gain a deeper understanding of the nature of others, and the relationships with these individuals will flourish because they will understand that you have taken the time to give, care, and understand their true nature and driving force, and for that, you will be possessing a rare priceless quality in this day and age.

If you can increase your ability to read personalities, understand individuals likes and dislikes, and realize the motivations of individuals in your relationships, you will better understand the nature of others. When you have developed a better relationship with yourself and better understand the nature of those with whom you share a relationship, your relationships will begin to enter a realm of lasting prosperity. These two points are the foundation of great relationships. The remaining solutions to reaching a prosperous relationship deal more with personal attributes, attributes that will enable you to fine-tune your relationship skills, continually improving the quality of your life and the lives of those who share relationships with you.

COMMUNICATION

Communicating your feelings effectively in relationships is one of the most important parts of a successful relationship. If a relationship lacks in proper communication it will be doomed to unresolved emotions. When we do not have the ability to communicate and tell the truth about how we feel in relationships, we have a tendency to become frustrated, stand offish, and to develop bad habits causing more tension to an already brittle relationship. One great thing about a healthy relationship is the ability to speak your mind without fear, to vent your daily frustration allowing the frustration to pass through your body quickly. When there is a lack of communication we are never able to speak our minds freely, ever conversation becomes reserved because you are constantly aware of what not to say. Daily frustrations become built up with no release because you are afraid to speak your mind freely and vent. These built up frustrations eventually lead to the abuse of yourself and others; abuse such as mental, physical, and drug & alcohol to name a few.

It is imperative that proper communication is developed in your relationships. If your spouse is doing things that are upsetting you then tell them exactly what it is they are doing and how it is making you feel. If you have a friend that is bothering you, then tell them exactly how you feel and exactly what it is they are doing to make you feel that way. When you can open up and tell these people how you really feel, you can have a relationship free of unsaid frustrations. The problem is many people are scared to speak their mind to people they share relationships with, they are afraid of upsetting them, afraid they might run out and leave, or maybe they are afraid they will be abused. The fact of the matter is, honesty is the best policy and whenever true feeling is spoken and laid on the table, there is nothing left to hide. Tensions can be released, leaving these individuals to reply back, get upset, or go into a rage. Generally, when you call someone on things that you feel are causing you concern, they have a tendency to vent their own concerns back to you. Your candid truths will allow the relationship to open the door to honesty allowing each to vent their frustrations in a healthy manner. For example, in a spousal relationship the husband may tell the wife that something she is doing is driving him crazy and has been for quite sometime, and she may reply by mentioning to him that he is doing something that is driving her crazy. He may not have even had an idea that the particular thing he was doing was driving her crazy and causing her frustrations, but because he decided to communicate how he felt, he was able to open up the relationship and have that openness reciprocated onto him enabling them both to shed some frustrations.

The key to communicating effectively is not to be brash. If you are frustrated and it has been built up for a while, try to calm your feelings before you begin to shed your frustrations. Approach the other party as smoothly as you possibly can. Do not barge in with cut downs and criticism for this only primes you and the one you are communicating with for an anger and an argument. Communicating your frustrations and desires is not designed to start arguments; it is designed to prevent them. Remember that the feelings you give you are likely to get in return, so when you get ready to communicate with someone about your frustrations and desires, do it nicely, Use kind words in calm tones and present your problem with an intent for understanding.

Only when things are perfectly open in a relationship can they begin to grow and maximize to their fullest potential. By communicating your true feelings and desires to those you are in relationships with, you can open the door to honesty and lose any inhibitions and reservations. When a relationship is based on communication and honesty; happiness and prosperity are sure to follow.

CONFIDENCE & TRUST

A helpful ingredient to possessing successful relationships is to have confidence in yourself and the ones you are in a relationship with. Confidence in the fact that you feel certain that you can maintain a successful relationship and you feel certain that the individuals in relationships with you can maintain successful relationships. With confidence comes trust in a relationship, trust is very important, for with out it there is nothing. If you cannot trust the ones you share relationships with then there is no relationship. Relationships are designed to strengthen, support, motivate, and create a sense of unity between two people, when there is no trust, none of these things can exist.

Many individuals are living in non-trusting relationships blaming on the ones they are in relationships with, when in fact it is a lack of trust and confidence in ones own capabilities. If an individual does not have confidence and trust in their own ability to have lasting, caring, loving relationships, how can they have trust and confidence in someone else to feel that way towards them? For example, if you have trouble trusting your spouse, it may be the fact that you lack the confidence in your ability to please your spouse, maybe spiritually, financially, or sexually. With that being the case, you should first learn to trust yourself and have confidence in your abilities to feel that you can make your spouse content with only you in their life. The majority of the time, non-trusting is derived from within and the feeling is transferred to others you are sharing relationships with. When you have total trust and confidence in your ability to please others, you will gain trust and confidence in their ability to feel pleased when they are in your presence.

The next time you find yourself overwhelmed with non-trusting emotions, be sure to check the feelings you have about yourself at that particular moment. Chances are, you will find yourself with low-esteem, lacking in trust for your own abilities to please others. Until there is concrete proof for you not to trust another in a relationship, you will be much better off to allow yourself to trust that individual fully until they do something official for you not to trust them. For example, if you happen to stumble upon your spouse at lunch with and ex-girlfriend or boyfriend, that is something concrete to base a feeling of non-trust and the matter should be confronted accordingly, but if you are only speculating that something like this is going on based on your own insecurities, then that is something non-concrete and should be effectively removed from your relationship by learning to gain trust and confidence in yourself and your relationship abilities. Completely trusting yourself will give you the confidence to completely have confidence and trust in others, allowing your relationships to grow richer and prosperous.

PATIENCE

Patience is a valid virtue to successful relationships. Understand, successful relationships do not happen overnight and they do not come without hardships. Anything worth doing in your life does not come without effort and patience. When you begin the task of improving your relationships, remember to have patience in yourself and the ones you share relationships with. If you find yourself having trouble developing a positive inner relationship, or communicating effectively, or having confidence and trust in yourself and others, just be patient and work your way through it. If you allow frustration to enter your mind, it will become extrimly difficult to make a positive change in your life. Frustration causes clouded vision and drains the body of energy, which eventually leads to quitting the cause of your frustration. Anytime you make a change within yourself, you are going up against many years of a particular pattern, and any time you attempt to change that pattern you will be confronted with an initial retaliation against change. The problem is, no matter if the pattern is positive or negative, your body has become comfortable with it in your life, hence the reason it is considered a pattern. By changing the comfortable pattern your body will put up sub-conscious resistance in fear of an unknown change, even if the change is going to be positive, the fact that it is unknown and new causes the resistance. The way to beat this reaction is to understand what is taking place and why it is taking place. When you are in the midst of bettering your relationships and find yourself reverting back to your old ways, let frustration pass you by and take a few moments to analyze the situation. If you can say to yourself, "I know I should not have said that or reacted that way, this change is difficult because I have been reacting this way for so long, but I am confident if I stay the course I will eventually accomplish this successful change", instead of saying "Why am I so stupid, I always put my foot in my mouth, I always over react, I am going to be this way for the rest of my life, I should have known trying to make a positive change would be impossible for me." The difference between dialogues is that the first dialogue will breed patience, persistence, understanding, and success, while the second dialogue will breed frustration, confusion, and failure. Understand that change is not easy and having patience with yourself will allow you to prevail and accomplish.

The same goes for those you share relationships with. When you become frustrated with the individuals in relationships you are trying to improve, just remember how hard it was for you to make a change and be patient with their reactions. Again, a lack of patience in the improving process will allow you to become frustrated, confused, and angered which leads to clouded vision, bad reactions, and failure. Be patient with these individuals and stay the course. When you can remain patient with another and remain on the course to positive change, they will eventually understand what it takes to improve. By witnessing your patience and calm persistence with them, they will gain a sense of patience and persistence of their own to make a positive change. The more patience one can posses internally the more patience they can transpose to another, and the more patience you can transpose to another, the more understanding they will have of the challenges they face to make a positive change in their life. So, remember to be patient with yourself and the changes you are making, and be doubly patient with the individuals in your relationships and the improvements they are attempting to make.

LISTENING

A great tool, which is vital to successful relationships and it is often never used, is called listening. Listening involves saying noting at times, expressing no judgment or opinions, simply just hearing clearly what others are saying. Many of us often overlook this skill. If you are trying to achieve success in your relationships, the skill of listening is an attribute that must be obtained. Many failed relationships are the direct result of individuals not listening to one another. Listening to the things that make the other individuals happy, sad, upset, frustrated, and angry. Listening to their goals and dreams, and their everyday wants and needs. When we do not properly listen to one another, we often miss important information and action on that information is never taken.

Listening like anything else is a skill that can be acquired. We must first understand why it is difficult for many of us to listen properly. In this day and age, we are all taught to care primarily for our own needs and our own feelings, this manner of thinking puts us in an entirely self centered mode, where everything revolves around you and your feelings. When this occurs we are left with sub-conscious thought of our selves only, so if someone is in conversation with you, and the conversation does not pertain to you or your interest we suddenly begin to go into a blocking out mode. I like to call it a blocking out mode, because this is the point where you block out all that is being said because it is not about you or your interest. It is the point where you either begin thinking of what you want to say next, or day dreaming of something else you would rather be doing. When this occurs all that is coming through your ears and into your mind is noise. Some individuals self centered blocking out mode is more apparent than others, I am sure you have met someone who never lets you get a sentence in because they are always speaking over you or interrupting you just as you are about to speak, or the individuals who say, "huh, what did you say", after you just spilled your heart out to them. These reactions are examples of the blocking out mode. Some people can hide their blocking out mode a little better than others, but the tendency to posses the blocking out mode is in all of us. The more you can understand that poor listening is derived from a self-centered nature, the more your listening skills will improve. By understanding the nature of the problem, you will have a better grasp on why you are blocking others out and how to correct the bad habit.

When you have understood the root of the problem you can begin to test your listening skills in relationship situations. Now that you understand that the roots of non-listening are derived from within, you can begin to make a conscious recognition when your blocking out mode occurs. The next time you are in conversation with a spouse or a friend and the conversation is not about you or your interest, but it is an interest to them, keep a keen internal ear to your thoughts. If you find yourself wanting to interrupt and turn the conversation to something you want to talk about or you find yourself deep in thought of what you are going to say as soon as they stop talking, then your blocking out mode has begun and at this time you need to red flag your reaction and begin to quiet down externally and internally and listen completely to what the other individual is having to say. When you can consciously

121

recognized that your blocking out mode is occurring, you will be able to cure the problem. Many people never even realize why or when their blocking out mode is taking place, leaving their life filled only with self-centered thoughts, which eventually leave these individuals empty, lonely, and lacking in successful relationships, because no one wants to be around someone who is not going to listen to them or someone who is going to interrupt their ever word.

There are times in our life when talking is far less important than listening. By learning to listen effectively, you can make your ears great teachers and they can become an excellent asset in your life. When we listen properly, we learn more, more of the world we live in and more of the people that live in it. Listening is something that needs to be done with out any thoughts of your opinions or judgments on the matter, simply just taking in what the other is saying and feeling with no thought of how you feel about it or what you think about. If you feel a relationship is not reaching its potential make sure that your listening skills are functioning properly. Listening is another attribute that is reciprocated, so the more you listen quietly to others without any internal mental interruptions or external interrupting others, you will find yourself receiving the same reactions when it is your turn to speak. Good listening skills are contagious, the more your listening skills improve, the more you will want to listen to others, and the more others will feel you are listening to them, and the more they will want to improve their listen skills to better listen to you. Listening in a relationship is of the highest importance, it is virtually impossible for a relationship to grow prosperous and healthy without proper listening being a large part of that relationship. So now is the time for you to begin to understand where your listening habits derived from and consciously recognize when your blocking out reaction is occurring and correct that reaction. When you accomplish this, your listening skills will improve and your relationships will become successful.

PRIDE

Pride can be a major deterrent in relationships. Pride to a certain degree can be a good thing in our lives, but if misunderstood, it can be a relationship killer. The ability to take pride in yourself and feel good about yourself, the things you have, and the things you are accomplishing is a good thing. Pride becomes negative when moderate pride turns into excessive pride. Excessive pride to the point where no one, even those closest to you, can tell you wrong and a feeling that you are never wrong or a feeling that you should ever have to apologize for your actions, and never showing emotions in a fear of showing weakness. Someone who is filled with too much pride is someone who gets angry and ignores the comments of those they share relationships with when they are trying to tell them of something they need to work on or a positive change they need to make. Being over filled with pride, these individuals take these constructive comments as a bash on their wonderful character and wonder, "how dare they say such things, do they not know how wonderful I am?" Someone with too much pride possesses a feeling of never being wrong even if they are. If a disagreement is at hand in one of their relationships, the other individuals point of the disagreement will often go ignored or discredited, for the individual with too much pride, it will be considered an attack on their undefeated record of being right, because they are never wrong, their pride will not allow them to be wrong. An individual possessing too much pride is never able to apologize for their negative actions towards others, even if the apology will cure the pain of the one who was treated negatively. The individuals who have excessive pride may feel they treated someone negatively, but their excessive pride will never allow them to make an apology because they feel if they apologize, they will be admitting that they were wrong. Eventually their excessive pride will turn them into a person who cannot show their true emotions in a relationship, due to fear of portraying some form of weakness.

If you feel you are in need of a pride reduction, look at the way you behave when you are in conversations or confrontations. If you are in fear that you can never be wrong or you can never apologize for bad behavior, then chances are you need to check your pride at the door. The truth is, no one is perfect, we are all wrong at times, and we all behave negatively at times. The key is to realize that it is okay to be wrong and it takes a stronger person who can admit when they are wrong and apologize when they are in the wrong. When you can let go of your fear of having the notion to always be right no matter the situation and the fear of never showing your remorse to others for your negative wrong doings, you will be able to take control of your pride and maintain it at a positive level. There is nothing wrong with feeling pride for yourself and your accomplishments, but when it reaches a point of feeling untouchable and uncorrectable, pride needs to be reduced in your life. To maintain prosperous healthy relationships it is much better to have less pride to where you can apologize and admit you are wrong than to have too much pride where you will never admit you are wrong or never apologize for your wrong doings. People do not want to spend there time with someone who is never wrong or can never say they are sorry. They want to spend their time with someone who is human, someone who can admit they are wrong and apologize when they are.

FEAR OF SHOWING EMOTIONS

Someone who cannot show their true emotions is someone who is doomed to never have prosperous successful relationships. The first thing to losing your fear of showing emotions is to lower the levels of pride in your life. When you lower your pride, you become more open to showing your true emotions to others. Many people out there are completely afraid of showing any type of pride in their life in fear they will portray weakness. The irony to this is they are portraying a much greater weakness by never being able to show their true emotions to others. There are individuals who cannot cry in front of others; mothers and fathers who cannot tell their own daughters and sons that they love them; managers who cannot give compliments to their subordinates; and spouses who cannot express true physical emotion to their partner, such as holding hands, hugging, or a kiss. Successful relationships will never occur in these individual's lives until they lose the fear of showing emotions.

To accomplish this, these individuals must lower their pride; to a point where they are not afraid to show others that they have made them experience sadness, love, or happiness. Another way to get over the fear of showing emotions is to stop caring what others will think of you if you portray your true emotions. A lot of the fear of showing emotions comes from individuals being too concerned with what others will think of them. They are afraid to cry over something sad in fear others will think they are weak. These individuals are afraid to tell others they love them in fear others will think they are now in control and try to take advantage of that control. They are afraid to express their happiness and compliments to others in fear that others will gain too much confidence and change on them. They are in fear of telling others how they really feel in fear that they will scare people away, afraid of expressing their true self in fear that others will not accept them. All this fear of showing emotions eventually consumes their entire life, leaving these individuals being thought of as very dry, hard, too cool, standoffish, mysterious, shy, and tough. When in fact these individuals are scared, timid, soft, misunderstood, confused, in need of help, closed off from any true happiness, and full of false pride.

The fact of the matter is, the size of an individual can be measured by the emotions they are able to portray to others, and the success of a relationship is highly dependent on the emotions each individual can portray to the other. If you feel you are incapable of showing your true emotions to others caused from an internal fear, then it is time to simply let go. Let go of your pride, and let go of the fears you have of what others will think when you express your true self. After all, what is a relationship if someone never truly knows the real you because you cannot express your true self? How can you ever be sure these relationships are real if individuals never get to see the real you. Why would you want a relationship with someone if you feel they cannot accept the real you? The point it becomes real and a relationship becomes successful is when you can muster up the courage to lay it all on the line and express your true emotions to the ones you have relationships with. The ones that accept you for who you really are and the person you are not afraid of being are the ones who are worthy of a true relationship. You are better off being completely alone and true to yourself and your real emotions than having everyone around you in superficial relationships with a person you are not or being a person that is afraid to be real. Your relationships only become prosperous when you can show your true emotions to others and only then will your relationships become real and you become true to yourself and others giving each other the confidence to express their true emotions.

RESPECT

Having respect for the individuals in your relationships is an excellent way to increase the prosperity of your relationships. When you have respect for the people you share relationships with, you have a tendency to treat those individuals in the manner in which they desire to be treated. A relationship where respect is involved is a relationship prone for prosperity and joy. A relationship without respect is a relationship prone for disaster and hardship. If you do not respect the individuals in your relationships, then the relationship can never develop mutually to a level of success. By not respecting others, there is a tendency for constant mistreatment, verbally, emotionally, and sometimes physically. Many failed relationships are the result of a lack of mutual respect between the two. Generally, the lack of respect begins with one and is reciprocated to the other. A relationship may start out with one individual respecting the other but the other individual does not have respect in return. Eventually this lack of respect will cause both individuals to have a lack of respect for one another. If one person is respecting the other and the other is mistreating that respect by not respecting them in return, the constant mistreatment will cause the other to begin acting in the same manner and it becomes a relationship based on disrespect. If you feel there is no hope for you ever respecting a particular individual you are in a relationship with, then you need to rectify the situation by possibly letting go of that relationship because people are better of alone than being treated with disrespect and abuse. You see if you do not respect someone then you will be treating him or her with disrespect, and disrespect is in direct correlation with abuse.

Proper respect for others can be obtained by using internal mental restructuring. Mental restructuring by understanding that respect comes from focusing on individual's positive qualities and disrespect is derived from focusing on individual's negative qualities. Also by learning to respect someone unconditionally and indefinitely, and by understanding what it means to use a dialogue based on respect versus a dialogue based on disrespect.

Many relationships start out with respect and adoration for the other and over the course of time when you begin to know these individuals more, the respect and adoration you previously had for that individual may be taken for granite and a pattern of disrespect may occur, where you only focus on those individual's negative qualities. When you respect someone, you respect everything about him or her, their opinions, beliefs, values, morals, past, the way they dress, and the way they look, you respect them unconditionally. For example, if you once found your spouse beautiful and sexy, but over the years, they have gained a few pounds and your attraction for them has decreased you may sub-consciously begin to decrease your respect for them. Eventually this will lead to abuse, and mistreatment deteriorating the relationship day by day. If you find a similar pattern like this occurring in your life, it is important to understand that disrespect should never be maintained in a relationship. For the sake of this example, lets say your attraction for your spouse has decreased because they have gained weight, instead of constantly focusing on their negative appearance and eventually losing respect for them causing you to become abusive and disrespectful, try to focus on the positive person they are and focus on the person they can become. When you can focus properly on their good qualities you will be able to maintain your respect for them and solve the problem that is causing you discomfort effectively. Understand that when you lose respect for an individual say your spouse, you begin a cycle of mistreatment, constantly abusing the other because you are venting your frustrations of them sub-consciously. This abuse causes the other to lose more respect for their selves and eventually lose respect for you, which will cause them to never become motivated to make a positive change. If anything the problem will only get worse because their sub-conscious will want to retaliate to the mistreatment they have experienced from you. For example, if your spouse has gained too much weight they may sub-consciously want to continue gaining more weight to cause you more pain for the pain you are causing them, due to the disrespect you have for them. When you can focus on the other individual's positive qualities such as your spouse, you can change the cycle of disrespect and abuse. Instead of losing respect for your spouse becoming overweight, you should continually respect them trying to give them positive encouragement to want to improve. Use positive respectful dialogue saying things such as, "honey, I love you and respect you dearly and I always will unconditionally, but the weight you are gaining is causing me frustration and causing me to be concerned for your health", "if there is something frustrating you causing you to abuse your body, please let me know so I can help", "I know how beautiful your figure used to be and I know it can continually look that way for the rest of your life you just have to work a little harder at it when you get a little older", "so please with my help try to work on it for me." Now this may sound a little harsh, but is a dialogue based on respect and this type of dialogue has a much greater success rate than the alternative of saying, "babe, have you looked at yourself in the mirror lately", "do you know how fat you are getting", "people are starting to comment on your obesity," "you are totally turning me off", "if you do not lose some weight I am leaving." This is a dialogue based on disrespect, one that uses harsh words damaging an individual's confidence and motivation with no regard. The point is taken in both dialogues, but the dialogue based on respect will cause the other to admire the way you are handling the matter and realize you still respect them when they are at a low point in their life. Sensing your devote respect for them will aid in their motivation to help them make a positive change in their life causing the relationship to grow stronger than ever before. The dialogue based on disrespect is one that causes the other to begin feeling inferior due to harsh words and mistreatment, losing self- respect and losing respect for you in the process. A loss of self respect and respect in you will only cause their problem to become worse, never gaining the proper motivation to make a positive change. The relationship will eventually deteriorate to constant misery and abuse. So, make sure to maintain constant unconditional respect in your relationships, which will allow you to use positive dialogue with others, increasing your happiness and increasing the happiness of those you share relationships with.

BODY LANGUAGE

Improving your body language is a simple tool that can improve your relationships. The impression others have of you depends somewhat on your body language, things such as, your posture, eye contact, handshake, facial expressions, the way you show affection to others, and the way you walk. Improving your body language is accomplished by simply making an effort to be aware of your body language in the presence of others. Realize if you are using correct posture by allowing your spine to remain fully erect giving the presence of energy and confidence, make sure you are not slouching which gives off the presence of tiredness and low-esteem. When you are talking to someone, check yourself to make sure you are making direct eye contact with that individual to give the presence of attentiveness, interest, and assertiveness, make sure you are not looking away or roaming your eyes away from the individual your are in conversation with, because it gives the appearance of not listening or passiveness. Realize the firmness of your handshake when you are meeting someone. Is it too soft? Is it too hard or is it just right? The impression of a handshake can leave someone thinking you are a timid individual if it is too soft or an overly aggressive individual if it is too hard; so practice perfecting the handshake with someone you know. Try to recognize your facial expressions when you are in the presence of others, do you have a tendency to smile and look happy giving a presence of contentment, confidence, and success or do you have a tendency to droop and frown giving a presence of unhappiness and failure? The way you show your affection is an important part of a loving relationship. It is important to not to be overly dry, never being able to give a hug and kiss, or never being able to hold hands without being embarrassed. If you are in a loving relationship, it is important to physically express to the other how you feel. Do not be afraid to give them a loving hug and kiss everyday or walk through a park holding hands. Remember, it takes a stronger, more confident individual to be able to express their true feelings. Realize that how you walk is sometimes a perception of how you feel about yourself. When you are walking, try to recognize if you have any style and confidence in your walk, if so great, and if you do not try to work on personalizing a strut, to increase your presence of internal confidence.

Realizing your body language when you are among others is an excellent way to increase your relationships prosperity and success. By improving your body language, you will increase the perception individuals have of you, and increase the confidence you have in yourself.

AVOIDANCE

Learning the art of avoidance can be a great asset in ones life. There are certain relationships that people maintain with individuals who do not bring out their best attributes and it is a proven fact that the people who you associate with can have a direct link to your over happiness and success. If there are relationships that you possess with individuals who bring the worst out in you, they need to be restructured and if these relationships cannot become restructured, they need to be avoided. Say if there is someone, you share a relationship with and all you two seem to do when you get together is abuse alcohol or drugs and there is no hope of ever enjoying anything else together, then that relationship needs to be avoided at all cost. If there is an individual who constantly makes you feel bad when you are around them, even after exhausting attempts to change the relationship, then the relationship needs to be avoided. If you are in a marriage that has deteriorated over many years and there is no hope for reconciliation then this relationship must cease to exist and be avoided as much as possible. The art of avoidance can help make your life more successful. You see there are certain people who bring the best out in us and make us feel good and there are certain people who bring the worst out in us and make us feel bad. Surrounding yourself with individuals who bring the best out in you will increase your chances of success and happiness. Now I am not saying to start ignoring everyone who makes you feel lousy at times, I am simply trying to help you understand that some relationships aid us in reaching our full potential while others work against our potential. The negative relationships that should be avoided are the ones that you have given a true, honest, fare, chance to try to become successful and prosperous; the ones that have had countless years of negative counter action causing no happiness to either party; the ones that you have great time, energy, and effort invested in changing to the positive with no avail; the ones that have never progressed positively over time or regressed to a point of no return, a point of no return where all the two of you can think of is your previous negative occurrences; the relationships you feel may cause a problem with another your more important relationships, if you are married, it can be a girlfriend/boyfriend, ex-lover, or someone you feel an uncontrollable attraction for. If you are happily married, there should be no reason to fulfill these desires, so for the sake of your relationship with your spouse it would be in your best interest to avoid these individuals. Strategic avoidance can bring added pleasure to your life, while maintaining negative relationships can bring added misfortune to your life. In the art of avoidance, it should not just be an avoidance of certain individuals, but an avoidance of certain things that bring the worst out in you as well. For example, if you have a negative relationship with alcohol to where every time you get near it something bad happens, then it should be avoided. If there is something you do that causes you to behave negatively then it needs to be avoided. For example, I remember there was a time in my life when I was very serious about playing golf, I had a negative relationship with the game, I would get incredibly angry on the course, if I played poorly it would hurt my self-esteem and ruin the rest of my day and evening. One day I realized the game was bringing more negative to my life than positive and I felt I needed to take a break and I avoided the game for a while until I could gain a better perspective on the game. The moment I began to avoid it, I found myself feeling better, sleeping better, and getting more of my self-esteem back. After a good dose of avoidance I was able to return to the game with a new, casual perspective and truly learned to enjoy the game whether I was playing good or bad.

A proper perspective in your life of whom and what you need to avoid is definitely an asset to anyone's happiness. So, analyze who and what causes you more grief than pleasure. If you feel it can be repaired without avoidance then give it a try, but if it remains as a constant negative factor in your life, then use the art of avoidance and give it a rest for a while until you gain a better perspective on them or it. Do not put a time constraint on the avoidance period let it be until you feel 100 percent confident you have a proper perspective of how to handle the matter, it could be a week or it could be indefinitely. However long it takes, I am confident there will be a gained sense of peace when you avoid the negative factions in your life.

VISUALIZING

As with any successful thing you desire in your life, it is important to have the ability to visualize it before it happens. If your mind has the ability to visualize something positive in your life then it can become a reality. I cannot stress enough, "that which you focus on your mind will draw closer to." If you are constantly focusing on how bad your life is and how negative and unhealthy your relationships are, then you are bound to stay unhappy and your relationships are bound to stay unhealthy. A great misconception derived from a deeper source is that when people visualize and focus on the negative aspects of their lives and the negative places it will lead them it is concrete fact and reality, but when they focus on positive aspects of their life and where they want their life to be, it is silly, childish, and dreamy. The truth is no matter what we visualize and focus on, whether positive or negative is a temporary dream, but the act of visualizing brings our life closer to that dream. So in essence, if you are visualizing negatively it is just as much a dream as visualizing positively. That means you have the ability to decide what you want to visualize, do you want it to be a visualization of a negative life filled with negative, unhealthy relationships or do you want it to be a visualization of a positive life filled with positive, healthy relationships? Therefore, if you want and desire positive prosperous relationships, take some alone time throughout the day and visualize the types of positive relationships you desire, not the negative relationships we all try to avoid. You can visualize the way you want current relationships to be and visualize the type of people you want new relationships with. If you can visualize these relationships being prosperous, healthy, respectful, encouraging, and bringing great pleasure and joy, then it can become reality. I am sure you have an idea of the type of relationships you desire with people, so visualize that idea, focus on it, and make it a reality. Visualize the way you see yourself looking, acting, and behaving in these relationships and the way you want others to look, act, and behave in these relationships. When you can turn your idea of the perfect relationship into a detailed visualization, you will have the ability to make a positive relationship change in yourself and those you share relationships with.

CONCLUSION

Relationships play an important role in our lives; they affect our happiness, success, and overall well-being. On the road to total prosperity, it is vital that you maintain happy, successful relationships in your life. Successful relationships with your spouse, parents, grandparents, kids, friends, peers, co-workers, bosses, and anything or anyone else you associate with. Successful relationships do not come easy; they require a great deal of care, effort, support, and energy from each individual in that relationship. The best thing to have on your side in the quest for successful relationships is a concrete understanding of what is required to obtaining healthy, successful relationships. For without understanding everyone is lost and confused. Making a blind attempt to repair something with no knowledge and understanding of the proper tools required in fixing the situation, but when this knowledge and understanding is obtained, there could be no mistake or wasted effort at repairing the problems. All the effort will be focused on the proper tools for the situation allowing for the maximum time and rate of success. The first step to having a concrete understanding of what it takes to maintain successful relationships is an understanding of the importance of developing a healthy, positive internal relationship within you. An understanding of the importance of an internal successful relationship allows you to gain a better understanding of the importance of being able to realize, see, and understand clearly the true nature of others and the importance understanding the nature of others has on the success and happiness of relationships. Once a full understand has been developed of the importance of your own internal relationship and an understanding is developed of the dependence on knowing the nature of others has to the success of your relationships, you can then begin to fine tune your relationship skills by better understanding the importance communication; confidence and trust; patience; listening; pride; losing the fear of showing emotions; respect; body language; avoidance; and visualizing happy, successful relationships; has on your ability to maintain happy, successful, prosperous relationships for a life time. When an understanding of what it takes to develop successful relationships is grasped, the sky is the limit. When you begin to implement your understanding of the requirements of successful relationships upon your own relationships, you will begin to see the true benefits of positive, prosperous relationships in your life. Healthy relationships can bring great joy, increased energy, support, comfort, peace, success, added confidence, and happiness in your life. When your relationships become successful, they lead you to the road of total prosperity.

Know thyself and succeed!!

CHAPTER 6

DIET

YOUR DIET PLAYS AN IMPORTANT role in your life. Diet can be thought of as many things, what you eat, what you desire to eat, how you eat, and how often you eat are some examples of diet. Our diets are the source of what gives us energy, make us feel and look healthy, and are directly linked to our life expectancy. The importance of the relationship between your diet and your success must not go overlooked. A proper diet in your life can make you stronger while a negative diet can destroy you. It is impossible to achieve total prosperity in your life without a proper diet. There are individuals out there who may have the money, the big house, the nice cars, the good job, but they have not incorporated a proper diet in their life. Nevertheless, many individuals will still look upon this person as being as close to total prosperity as you would ever want to be, but that is far from the truth. These less than prosperous individuals have to live with the garbage they are feeding themselves everyday, and for that, they are more than likely fighting obesity, putting their health in risk, and constantly fighting fatigue. These individuals have not achieved total prosperity or anything remotely close to because they have to look in the mirror everyday and not feel proud of what they see looking back at them, nor are these individuals experiencing what it feels like to live a day maximizing the potential of their physical and mental well-being caused from a proper diet. How can one have achieved total prosperity when they are not fully confident in their appearance and the obese creation staring at them in the mirror and they do not know what it feels like for the mind and body to function properly and efficiently which is subsequently derived from a healthy diet? If these individuals could only realize that the food they eat is their fuel source, and just as a sports car with a powerful engine will not run to its performance potential with bad fuel running through it, a highly sophisticated human body cannot function to its performance with unhealthy food intake. Maybe if the individuals who possessed negative eating habits realized every time they ate negatively they were fueling their body to function improper, gain fat, promote anxiety, have a minimal supply of energy, and decrease their life expectancy, they would think twice about ignoring a proper diet and discrediting the importance proper eating habits has on the human bodies performance. Our eating habits are a vital role to reaching total prosperity and should never be ignored or discredited. If your goal in life is to one day live in health and happiness, possessing total prosperity then it is imperative you incorporate a healthy diet as a part of your life. For the goal of reaching total prosperity can never be attained without proper eating habits. Achieving total prosperity is like putting together a complicated puzzle and if one piece is missing from that puzzle, it will always be incomplete. Without every aspect of total prosperity functioning together as a team, then total prosperity can never be achieved. So, if you are serious about the desire to experience total prosperity in your life then I suggest you get serious about the importance of a proper diet in your life. Not to worry, if you feel your diet is not up to par, they can be improved, and when the improvement is made, the results will be felt and seen. You can begin to improve your diet by understanding what consist of a proper diet, and what can be defined as a negative diet and a positive diet and how to change those diet habits by learning to respect yourself. When you begin the task of improving your diet habits, you can implement simple solutions that will aid in your goal of a positive diet. You can then continually improve your diet habits by gaining a better knowledge of proper eating by fully understanding the food guide pyramid. When you begin to understand how much better your life can become with proper eating habits you will begin to wonder how you ever got by on negative eating habits. By improving your daily diet, you will be improving every other aspect in your life, which will allow your life to enter into the optimum zone of happiness and prosperity.

UNDERSTANDING EATING HABITS

You can begin to improve your diet by increasing your understanding of what eating habits are and what they consist of. Your eating habits consist of what you eat, when you eat, how you eat, how often you eat, how much you eat, and the foods you crave. When you begin to understand eating habits and the eating habits you posses, you can begin to improve on them in the areas improvement is needed.

What do you eat? Fore the sake of your health you need to ask yourself this question. The saying, *you are what you eat,* holds true. What you eat throughout the day is your fuel source, your energy supply so to speak. The food you put through your highly sophisticated body, daily, is the main energy supply you will be working on throughout the day. By simply gaining the knowledge of knowing exactly what you eat will give you better insight to the result of how you are feeling. Many people have no clue what they eat, they simply get hungry and fill the hunger craving at the point of there nearest convenience. When the day is done, these individuals will often times not even remember what they had for breakfast. They have overlooked the importance of knowing what they eat or they have never known the importance of knowing what they eat. When you are trying to improve your eating habits, it is important that you know exactly what you eat. When you can maintain a direct recollection of what you eat you can begin to assess what needs to be implemented in your diet and what needs to be removed from your diet.

When do you eat? Understanding this question is as important as understanding what you eat. Here again, there are many individuals who find food whenever their hunger cravings begin. They simply get hungry and they let their stomach guide them to food; any place, anytime. When the day is done they haven't the slightest recollection of when they ate, all they know is they got hungry and satisfied that hunger. To avoid becoming an individual who is a blind eater being lead by the seeing eye dog known as hunger cravings, it is important to understand that there are times throughout the day when our bodies are prime to digest food and turn that food into energy more efficiently and more healthy than others, and to make an improvement on the hours of the day you eat, it is important to know exactly when you have been eating. Having a direct knowledge of when you eat will allow you to make improvements on your eating schedule. Being able to answer the question when do you eat, allows you to understand exactly when you have been eating through out the day and when you know exactly when you have been eating throughout the day you can pinpoint with great accuracy the times of the day you need to improve on your eating habits and understand when you need to avoid food and when you need to find food.

How do you eat? Understanding this question will allow you to get the most out of your daily meals. How you eat consists of the manner or habit in which you eat. Understanding the manner in which you eat is very beneficial to improving your overall eating habits. To answer this question properly, it is important for you to become aware of the way you eat. To better understand how you eat, you need to become precise with your questions. Ask precise questions such as; when you eat, do you always eat on the run, never giving yourself a chance to enjoy the food you consume? When you eat, are you taking the time to chew your food properly giving allowing your digestive system to efficiently process your food with the least amount of energy or do you swallow the majority of your portions whole never giving your digestive system a chance to process the food you consume efficiently. When you eat, do you allow proper time for your meals to reach your stomach, allowing your stomach to function properly by giving it time to send impulses back to your brain telling you when you are full or do you engulf your food bombarding your stomach all at once never giving it time to function properly by sending impulses to your brain to tell you when you are full? When you can answer these questions, you can begin to understand how you eat. When you can fully understand how you eat, you can begin to fully understand the negative patterns you need to avoid when you are eating and the positive patterns you need to implement when you are eating.

How often do you eat? Knowing how often you eat is a major asset to proper successful eating habits. When you can ask, and properly answer this question to yourself you will have the knowledge to make positive changes in your daily eating routine. The questioning is point blank, how many times do you eat throughout the day, is it one, two, three, four, five, six? Many people often wonder why they are obese or under weight, without a clue that they are eating several extra meals than their body needs or not supplying enough daily meals to the calories their bodies are burning. To better improve your understanding of what consist of eating habits, it is important that you fully understand and are fully aware of how often you eat. If you are one of the individuals who gets too many hunger cravings throughout the day and constantly satisfies those cravings it is important to be aware of this. If you are one of the individuals who ignore one to many hunger cravings throughout the day it is important to understand that this is one of your eating habits. Odds are if you are obese you are eating too much and too many times throughout the day and odds are if you are under weight it is probably a direct result of you eating too small of portions and not enough meals throughout the day. When you fully know and understand how often you eat you can begin to implement of positive plan of attack to increase or decrease the amount of meals you are eating throughout the day to improve your eating habits.

How much do you eat? This is a simple question, but the only problem is many people avoid this question or never take the time to understand the importance this question has to their health. Understanding how much you eat will help you understand why you are fighting obesity or why you are constantly fighting to keep healthy weight on your body. Here again, many individuals will get a hunger craving and find a way to feed this craving, but without a proper understanding of how much they eat, they may find themselves feeding their hunger craving by feeding a craving that is enough for two people, or by feeding a craving that is not enough for a small child. Due to a lack of care or understanding of how much they eat, these individuals are simply constantly overeating or under eating, leading to obesity or malnutrition. It is important that you can fully answer the question; how much do you eat? When you can answer this question accurately, you will be able to make a positive improvement in your eating habits by adjusting the portion sizes you are feeding your cravings throughout the day.

What foods are you craving? Answering this question will allow you to understand and improve the cravings you are fighting throughout the day. When you ask yourself this question you will begin to understand some of your daily food motivations. For example, you may find yourself eating at the same restaurant everyday not for the healthy lunches they offer, but for the awesome apple cobbler they make for dessert. You may be aware of this food craving without a care of the negative consequences or this may be a sub-conscious craving leading you to this place daily never knowing why. The important thing to understand is that you become aware of your food cravings by asking yourself what your food cravings are. When you begin to understand your food cravings you can begin to understand the motivations you have for where, when, and why you are eating. You can then be able to understand where and why some of your daily energy and focus has been going to fight particular food cravings, and understand why it always leads you closer to them because of the energy and focus you have on them. Understanding your food cravings will allow you to assess which negative cravings you need to eliminate and which positive cravings you need to try to incorporate. So do not be afraid to honestly ask yourself what your food cravings are, for the answer may be surprising, but at least by knowing you can begin to make a positive improvement based on proper knowledge and understanding.

A better understanding of what eating habits consist of will allow you to positively improve on your diet. Our eating habits consist of what you eat, when you eat, how you eat, how often you eat, how much you eat, and the foods you crave. When you begin to personalize these questions and ask yourself what do I eat? When do I eat? How do I eat? How often do I eat? How much do I eat? What foods do I crave? When you answer these questions you can begin have a better understanding of yourself by better understanding why you feel the way you do, why your bodies energy levels are where they are, why you look the way you do, and why you find yourself eating at particular places and eating particular items. This better understanding of yourself and eating habits will enable you to set forth a definitive plan for positively changing your eating habits that will be engineered on proper knowledge and understanding of your personal eating habits, and an engineered plan of attack based on definitive knowledge and understand has a far greater chance of success than a plan of attack based on blind knowledge and understanding, because blind knowledge and a lack of understanding causes wasted effort, confusion, frustration, constant set backs, hopelessness, submission, and eventual failure. The more knowledge of eating habits and the personal eating habits you possess, the healthier, successful, and prosperous your eating habits will become.

UNDERSTANDING THE DIFFERENCE BETWEEN A POSITIVE AND NEGATIVE DIET & RESPECTING YOURSELF TO IMPROVE

In the quest to improve your diet, it is important to gain awareness between positive and negative eating habits. When you begin to form an understanding of a diet and eating habits associated with a diet, you begin to understand what your personal diet habits consist of. At this point, you can begin to determine if your personal eating habits are positive or negative. If you are in question as to whether an eating habit of yours is positive or negative, it is important to understand, concerning eating, that anything done in moderation is generally going to be better for you than anything done in excess. That being the case, the majorities of negative eating habits are very basic and require minimal knowledge to be able to distinguish between the two. Let me give you some examples of negative eating habits, there should be no question that someone who constantly over eats to the point where they feel incapacitated is in the midst of a negative eating habit. Someone who munches on high fat, high calorie, high sugar, snacks all day is in the midst of a negative eating habit. Someone who feels compelled to eat a heavy dessert with every meal is in the midst of a negative eating habit. Someone who eats there meals so fast they barely give themselves time to breath is in the midst of a negative eating habit. Someone who goes hungry most of the day only to eat one huge meal in the evening is in the midst of a negative eating habit. Someone who feels compelled to stop at the nearest fast food chain every time they get a hunger craving is in the midst of a negative eating habit. Someone who cannot control their cravings to overindulge in sweets and candies is in the midst of a negative eating habit. All the individuals who ignore or do not care what they eat, when they eat, how they eat, how often they eat, how much they eat, what foods they crave, how they feel when they eat negatively, what these negative eating habits are doing to their health, and how they look, are individuals who posses negative eating habits.

The better alternative is positive eating habits. Positive eating habits are not quite as easy to recognize as negative eating habits, but the more your understanding of eating habits grows the more these positive eating habits will become apparent and easily recognizable to you. Remember, anything done in moderation is generally going to be better for you than anything done in excess, especially concerning eating. Let me give you some examples of positive eating habits, someone who is fully conscious of the importance of what they feed their body possesses a positive eating habit. Someone who takes the time to chew slowly, fully taste their food, and give their stomach time to function properly by allowing the stomach to tell them when it is the right time to stop eating possesses a positive eating habit. Someone who eats three nutritional meals a day and snacks on healthy foods such as apples, carrots, nutritional shakes, or heath bars in between meals for added energy possesses a positive eating habit. Someone who does not allow themselves to eat late in the evening knowing their bodies will not burn it off with the best efficiency possesses a positive eating habit. Someone who has turned their negative food cravings into cravings for something healthy possesses a positive eating habit. Someone who will not eat something without fully knowing what that food consist of possesses a positive eating habit. Someone who does not ignore and overlook what they eat, when they eat, how they eat, how often they eat, how much they eat, and what foods they crave, possesses positive eating habits. Someone who wants to feel healthy and cares about their health understands that eating properly directly affects their health, which in turn motivates them to possess positive eating habits. Someone who cares about the way their body looks and respects themselves understands that what they eat affects how they look and by eating unhealthy they are disrespecting their body, will maintain positive eating habits. Someone who realizes that anything eaten in moderation is going to be better for him or her than anything eaten in excess possesses a positive eating habit.

You see knowing the difference between positive and negative eating habits is somewhat common sense. The majority of us know the foods that are bad for us and the foods that are good for us. What is important to understand concerning eating habits is that you can allow yourself to change negative eating habits by changing the way you think about these habits. For positive eating habits can be associated with positive thinking habits as well, because it is a state of mind. It is a cause and effect relationship. If you care and respect your body and health you are not going to allow yourself to eat negatively. When you respect yourself, you will in turn respect your body, your health, and your mind by incorporating a healthy diet in your life. It is virtually impossible to respect yourself and not respect the way you eat. When you do not fully respect yourself, it is much easier to not develop a healthy diet, because you do not have enough respect for yourself to care about the way you eat. Learning the importance of respecting yourself will allow you the ability to respect the way you eat. When you change your state of mind and begin to develop a well-rounded respect for yourself, your eating habits will follow the same pattern of respect and begin to improve. That is why diet is so important to reaching total prosperity. How can someone achieve total prosperity when they do not respect their body and health enough to eat healthy everyday? The answer is, they cannot. If you cannot change your state of mind and begin respecting your body and health, then obtaining a positive diet and total prosperity will be an impossible feat. When you learn to fully respect your body and health your mind will work in unison and automatically begin to focus on improving your diet for the sake of your body and your health.

SIMPLE SOLUTIONS

When you begin the task of improving your diet, there are simple solutions that exist to help you along the way. By following these solutions, your goal to achieve improved eating habits will become a reality. The simple solutions that will aid you on your journey of improving your diet include: setting real goals, taking it one step at a time, expecting setbacks, finding a role model, planning, reading, surrounding yourself with healthy foods, looking at the labels, improving your cooking, getting help, and rewarding yourself.

When you are setting the goal to improve your diet, it is important for the sake of your health mental and physical that you keep them realistic. Setting unrealistic goals can cause you to lose hope or go to desperate measures to try to accomplish these unrealistic goals. For example, take someone who is obese and has been eating negatively for many years, they decide to make an improvement on their eating habits and say, "I am going to eat as little as it takes to lose 30 pounds by the end of the month." What they do not understand is, this is an unhealthy, unrealistic goal. By setting this goal they are creating a motivation headed for disaster. They have put a narrow time constraint on themselves that leads to added pressure and they have set a very difficult number to achieve which creates extreme measures. These individuals will probably begin to starve themselves if they do not see fast results creating more unhealthy behavior, and when the goal is not achieved they will probably find themselves binge eating to feel the void of failure and the cravings they have been denying. By setting an excessive goal, they have created a situation where they have to implement excessive means to achieve this goal causing them to be excessive in their every action by either starving or bingeing. Nothing will be in moderation in these individuals eating habits, which will lead them to failure and possibly danger. When you begin to improve your eating habits be sure to set moderate realistic goals that will allow for the greatest chance of success.

When attempting to improve your eating habits, it is important to start out taking it one step at a time. Begin slowly until you have built up your confidence and discipline. When you begin to make improvements on your eating habits, do not put immediate time constraints and big numbers in your head. Simply break it down and take it slow. Start out by improving on the breakfasts that you eat and how you eat them until you have built up enough confidence that you have successfully improved on that meal. Then begin to work on the lunches that you eat and then move onto the dinners you eat. When you feel confident you have successfully improved your three daily primary meals, begin to improve on the snacks that you eat throughout the day and the cravings you have for negative foods. When you break down your diet into steps, you can successfully improve them. It is much easier to take on one than to take on one army. By attempting to improve every aspect of your diet overnight you will be going up against an army of negative diet habits and you will be heavily out numbered. The odds of success will be more in your favor to take them on one at a time until you have successfully mastered each.

By breaking down your eating habits into steps you can put all of your energy into that particular section until it is mastered, instead of breaking your energy up attempting to master all of your eating habits at once. When you have successfully master one step of your eating habits, you will have more momentum, knowledge, and confidence to master the other, eventually becoming an individual who possesses successful well-rounded eating habits.

When you begin the challenge of improving your diet, it is important to understand that it is just that, a challenge. Anytime we attempt to make a change in our lives it will come with some degree of challenge and difficult. The key is to understand this and to not allow frustration to control your mind when these life improvement challenges knock us down and set us back time to time. When you are facing a life improving challenge you are walking uphill and when you are not changing and remaining negative you are simply coasting downhill and remember, it is twice as hard and requires twice as much energy to walk uphill. So realize that no one is perfect and on your journey to improving your eating habits you will experience set backs and breakdowns from time to time. The key to your success will be how you handle these set backs. If you can be patient and learn from them, you will eventually prevail. For example, if your goal has been to lose ten pounds but every time you step on the scale it does not change or continues to go up, it is important to remain strong and focused and not allow frustration to break you down causing you to give up. If you can tell yourself, "Hey the body does not change overnight, I feel confident that if I continue on and give 100 percent of my effort to losing this ten pounds then it will eventually happen." Instead of saying, "This is hopeless, I have weighed my self for 4 weeks now and I have not changed a thing, all this hard work for nothing, I think I am just going to call it quits. To change your eating habits, try to remain positive and prepare yourself for set backs and difficulties and you will find your mind working on the correct path to success.

To give you inspiration on your journey to improving your eating habits, you should search for a role model to give you inspiration. If it is someone you know personally or someone you have heard about, try to find out as much about these individual as you can. Try to find out the way they think. Try to find out what motivates them, the setbacks they have experienced, how they succeeded in improving their eating habits, and the routines they follow. When you can learn more about these individuals success stories you can begin to implement them into your own life. During the challenge of improving your diet you may find yourself alone at times, as if you are the only person in the world trying to make such a difficult improvement in your life at the moment. This is not true, but the feeling of isolation can bring on uncertainty, confusion, and frustrations, leading you back downhill on the path to failure. To help break this feeling of isolation it is important to find a role model to emulate yourself after and to give you a sense of company during your challenge. Knowing that someone else has been through the same thing you are going through and has succeed will give you hope, security, and confidence to achieve the goal of improving your diet.

All challenges and goals in life are best overcome when there is a definitive plan of attack. Improving your easting habits can be accomplished more successfully and more efficiently when you have a well thought out plan. A well thought out plan for everything such as, a plan for what you are going to eat for breakfast, lunch, and dinner throughout the week. A plan for what you are going to buy at the grocery store. A plan for how you are going to handle your negative food cravings, and what healthy foods you can substitute for the negative food cravings. A plan for what you are going to snack on throughout the day. A plan for how you are going to handle set backs to your improvement phase. I think you get the idea. The better plan you have during your improving process the better prepared you will be for what's around the corner, and preparedness is what allows people to rise to the occasion and conquer our challenges. Therefore, when you get started on improving your eating habits set a descriptive plan and try to prepare yourself for everything. Remember the better your plan the better chance of success you will have at achieving your goal.

Reading all you can about nutrition and health will allow your knowledge of a healthy diet to grow. Reading on proper eating and nutrition will allow you to gain insight and understanding to the basics of proper eating habits such as, what foods to it and what foods to avoid, what are the healthiest ways to cook food, how to reduce your fat and cholesterol intake, and healthy alternatives to your negative food cravings. The more knowledge you have of what foods are healthy and what foods are not healthy the better your plan of attack can become. Anyone who has more knowledge on a subject than the others stands a much greater chance of succeeding than the other. For example, Tiger Woods does not dominate the PGA Tour on is raw talent alone, a great deal of his advantage over his competitors and the courses he plays is his profound knowledge of what it takes to make a golf ball do what he wants it to do. The same can hold true for individuals who are in perfect health and perfect shape, the advantage they have over others who are not in good health and good shape, is a deeper knowledge on what it truly means to eat healthy. If you want to defeat your negative eating habits, knowledge is your number one defense. By reading as much as you can in books, magazine articles, newspaper articles, web pages, etc... on proper eating habits and nutrition, you can gain the proper knowledge required to overcome negative eating habits. Search for the knowledge every chance you get and continue to grow wiser and learn to accomplish your goal of improving your diet.

A simple solution to help you get started eating more healthy is to surround yourself with healthy foods. The first place to start is your home. Keep your pantry and refrigerator stocked with healthy foods and try to minimize the amount of negative foods in your house. If someone you live with keeps unhealthy food around that you crave, have him or her put this food in a place that you will not look. When you have healthy foods at home, you will begin to take these healthy foods with you to work, allowing you to avoid fast food chains and vending machines. It is important to analyze the type of foods you are surrounded by and assess the changes that need to be made, because the foods we are surrounded by, we are more likely to eat. By learning to surround yourself with healthy foods instead of unhealthy foods, you will be one step ahead of the challenge of improving your eating habits.

Reading food labels is an excellent way to improve on your eating habits. If you are in question about a particular food whether it is good for you or bad for you, simply look at the label. It is a law now that all food products have a content label on them to fore warn the consumer of its negative contents. So, before you begin to eat something look at its contents label. If you have been fighting a negative craving for candy bars and cannot understand why you are constantly overweight, take a look at the content label on the back of a candy bar and maybe you will understand where the weight problem is coming from. When you develop the habit of looking at labels, you may be surprised at the contents of some of the foods you have been eating for many years. There may be foods you thought were good for you and are not and there may be foods you thought were bad for you but the label tells you otherwise. Reading labels is a way to unveil the truths in all foods and it can be a way to protect you from eating unhealthy foods. So if you are ever in question about a particular food read its content label, it will always tell you the truth and if you want to develop a positive habit that will aid in you goal to improve your eating habits, simply begin reading content labels on everything you eat.

Learning to cook healthy is another good solution to improve your diet. Many individuals have favorite foods that are healthy and good for them but they are cooking these foods in a way that is unhealthy. Learning to change the way you eat particular foods can improve your health. Lets take chicken and fish for example. If you fry chicken and fish or order chicken and fish fried every time you eat out, try to cook or order them cooked a different way. There are ways to cook and order foods that you enjoy, to change them from unhealthy to healthy such as learning to cook and order your foods broiled or grilled instead of fried. By simply changing your cooking and eating patterns to become healthier, you will be improving your diet greatly.

An excellent solution to improving your personal diet, which is often never visited, is to get help. Get help from a nutritionist, doctor, therapists, trainer, or whomever else you feel has profound knowledge of diet and nutrition. You can get help at anytime during the course of your improving process. You can find a professional before you get started to give you better knowledge and understanding or you can get help if you have been attempting to improve your diet for quite some time without any positive results and you should definitely get help if your frustrations are about to cause you to quit. Finding a diet and nutrition expert can help you in many ways, they can help you gain knowledge of how to accomplish your goal, increase your confidence, push you to achieve, and keep your efforts focused and efficient on the right course so there is no wasted energy. The only negative to a professional is that you may have to come out pocket a little, but how much do you value your health? Finding a diet and nutrition expert you feel comfortable with will increase your results rate greatly.

An excellent way to keep yourself motivated and confident when you are trying to improve your eating habits is to continually reward yourself. When you feel you have made progress on your goal, you should reward yourself for taking a step forward in a positive direction. The more you can reward yourself the more you will be able to remain positive and upbeat why you are accomplishing your goal to improve your eating habits. Reward yourself by giving yourself praise for taking a step forward and for your efforts, treat yourself to an nice meal, and allow yourself gratification by feeling proud of your accomplishment. When you begin to reward yourself for your positive actions, your mind will begin to focus on making positive improvements in your life. You see, because of the positive feedback and rewards you are giving yourself when you make an improvement or accomplish a goal your mind will sub-consciously gravitate toward more goal accomplishment in order to obtain the positive feelings you experience when you reward yourself. During your eating improvement process there will be plenty of negative feedback coming at you and it is important to always offset negative feedback with positive feedback. When you are consistently rewarding yourself you will produce consistent positive feedback to your eating improvements, and when you begin to receiving consistent positive feedback you will be putting yourself in excellent position for achievement, success and prosperity.

Implementing these simple solutions into your life is an excellent way to help you overcome negative eating habits. When you set out on the goal of improving your eating habits, it is going to be very challenging, but if you can weather these challenges and stay on the course to improvement and implement these helpful eating solutions, you will be successful in your goal of improving your diet.

FOOD GUIDE PYRAMID

In your quest of improving your diet, your success depends highly on your knowledge. Knowledge and understanding of diet and nutrition is a golden asset to healthy eating habits. It is virtually impossible to have too much knowledge of diet and nutrition and at the same time, there is a wide spread lack of knowledge of diet and nutrition throughout the world. A great way to improve your eating habits, your knowledge and the basics of diet and nutrition is to understanding the food guide pyramid. This pyramid can be your outline or blueprint of how you should pattern your daily meals. Most people have seen or at least heard of the food guide pyramid, but have never really taken the time to understand it, again maybe they purposely ignore their health, do not care about their health, or simply do not think it is important enough to worry about. Understanding the food guide pyramid is a knowledge that should not be taken lightly, for it tells you exactly what the body needs daily to function healthy, efficiently, and positively. The food guide pyramid looks like this:

Fats, Oils and Sweets — Meat, Poultry and Fish

Milk, Yogurt and Cheese — Fruit

Vegetables — Bread, Cereal, Rice and Pasta

This pyramid may look a little silly and cartoonish, but is far from a joke. This food pyramid was created by our United States Department of Agriculture and it is designed to give the common public building blocks for creating a healthy, balanced diet that includes all the nutrients needed to support and promote healthy living and healthy eating habits. Take some time too look at the food categories on the pyramid and see if these foods groups are recognizable in your home. The food groups include: fats, oils, and sweets; meat poultry and fish; milk, yogurt, and cheese; fruit; vegetables; and bread, cereal, rice, and pasta.

Fats, oils, and sweets should be taken very lightly. Examples for these can be the things you cook with such as cooking oil; the things you put on your foods for flavoring such as salts, salad dressings, and butter; and the sweets you enjoy such as candy bars, cakes, and pies. Fats, oils, and sweets are a required food source in the pyramid, but they should be used very sparingly. Our bodies need this for daily nutrition, just in much smaller amounts than the other food groups. Cutting down on your fats, oils, and sweets is a great way to start improving your diet.

Meat, poultry, and fish are our primary protein source. You are required to eat two to three servings of meat, poultry, or fish per day. One serving can be roughly described as three ounces. So six to nine ounces of meat, poultry, or fish is a healthy daily portion of this food group. When you are under or over that requirement, your body will not be able to function as efficiently as it would when you are eating the proper portion.

Milk, yogurt, and cheese are another food group that requires two to three servings per day. One serving of milk and yogurt is about one cup, and a serving of cheese is about one and one-half ounces. Here again it is important to use the proper daily portions if you want your body to function to its maximum potential. It is important to remember that milk, yogurt, and cheese are not described as a chocolate milkshake of frozen yogurt, because they are part of the sweets group. So use common sense and if you cheat, you will only be cheating yourself.

Fruits are a food group that you should be eating two to four servings per day. One serving can consist of about a one and one-half cup of fruit or about six ounces of fruit juice. Therefore, a twelve-ounce glass of orange juice and an apple can fill your daily quota. Fruits can also be an excellent replacement for the fats, oils, and sweets category. For example, you can put bananas in your cereal instead of sugar and eat something like apples, peaches, or tangerines for dessert instead of ice cream and cake.

Bread, cereal, rice, and pasta are our main carbohydrate food groups. They require about six to eleven servings per day. Roughly, one and one-half cup of cereal, pasta, or rice equal a serving and about a slice or one ounce of bread equals a serving. Therefore, a large muffin, one sandwich, and a pasta dish with a dinner role will fill your bread, cereal, rice, and pasta quota comfortably.

Vegetables require three to five servings per day. If you are eating leafy vegetables such as lettuce or spinach, about one cup should fill your daily quota. Vegetables such as carrots, corn, and green beans, slightly over a half of a cup will be sufficient. A six-ounce glass of vegetable juice such as tomato juice can also help you fill your daily quota.

When you begin to spend some time with the food guide pyramid and better understand the pyramid, your knowledge and your eating habits will begin to improve. Remember to eat six to eleven servings of the bread, cereal, rice, and pasta group; three to five servings of the vegetable group, two to three servings of the meat, poultry, and fish group; two to four servings of the fruit group; two to three servings of the milk, yogurt, and cheese group; and very sparingly use the fats, oils, and sweets group; everyday and your health and eating habits will improve drastically.

CONCLUSION

Proper diet is a very important part of people's lives. Your diet is a determining factor on how you feel, look, behave, and live. Improving your diet habits will help you improve all facets of your life such as your bodily appearance, your confidence level, your relationships, your financial success, and your overall happiness.

Diet habits or eating habits are something that must not go overlooked or ignored. It is important that you understand the importance your diet will have on determining if you reach total prosperity. An individual can never achieve total prosperity if they do not possess healthy eating habits. A healthy diet is directly linked to the respect you have for yourself and your body. Without a healthy diet, there can be no internal respect because how can someone continue to eat unhealthy realizing that they are destroying their own body and health, and in the process proclaim to have respect for their life and the body they live in? It does not make sense. With that in mind, how can someone ever achieve total prosperity if they do not respect themselves enough to eat healthy? Make it a point in your life to never overlook or ignore your eating habits again. When you give the importance of eating habits their proper respect, you will begin to put an emphasis on improving them. When the challenge of improving your diet begins, it will not come easy, but what things good in your life ever do? Improving your diet will require you to remain disciplined to the cause and focused on your achievement. Improvements on your eating habits can be done more efficiently and more successfully by gaining a concrete understanding of what consist of eating habits, when you can truly understand all that consist of eating habits you can begin to accurately judge your own eating habits; by learning what can be defined as negative eating habits and positive habits and how you can decrease your negative eating habits and increase your positive eating habits; by properly respecting yourself; by implementing and practicing   positive eating habit solutions into your life; and by fully understanding the importance and meaning of the food guide pyramid and incorporating the pyramid into you daily eating routine.   When your eating habit skills improve, you will begin to feel better about yourself and about your health.   When you improve your diet, you will be taking a direct action to the respect you have for your body and your health.   Only when you can take true action on your desires to improve due to a profound respect for yourself, will you be on the path to true total prosperity.

EAT TO LIVE, DO NOT LIVE TO EAT

CHAPTER 7

PHYSICAL HEALTH

PHYSICAL HEALTH IS A KEY ingredient of total prosperity. For happiness and success to be obtained, it is important that you use a great deal of effort to maintaining positive physical health. Physical health runs hand in hand with good eating habits because they both deal with taking proper care of your body and having proper respect for your body. It is not possible for someone to maintain positive physical health without maintaining positive eating habits. Physical health is merely an extension of healthy eating habits. When you incorporate healthy eating habits into your life, you will need to incorporate physical health in your life as well. If you have been eating negatively for many years, improving your eating habits will increase your health, but it will not be enough to erase the years of negative abuse that your body has taken, resulting in things such as heart disease, cellulose, softness, uncomfortable areas of body fat, weakness, poor cardiovascular maintenance, and inflexibility. The only way to totally improve the physical body is to incorporate positive physical health along with healthy eating habits. When you begin to incorporate positive physical health in your life, you can begin to make drastic improvements on your body increasing your vitality at the while. Only when action is taken and the physical training has begun can you begin to erase and improve on the negative factions your body has been fighting for years. Your physical health is just as important as anything else in your life and it should be given proper respect and recognition. Many individuals simply do not understand the importance of their physical health taking their bodies completely for granite. These individuals often times completely ignore the aspect of physical health or make a mockery to its importance and find their stomach over hanging their belt as amusing. This is very sad, because the human body is such a powerful thing and it is definitely something that should never be taken for granite or laughed at. The truth is, there is no humor to an unhealthy physical body. The fact that the human body is one of the most highly sophisticated creations known to science is evidence alone that the human body should never be mistreated. The government and all of it's scientist to this day, using billions of dollars, have not yet been able to invent any machine remotely close to the sophistication and efficiency the human body possesses. That fact only should make you realize that it is no laughing matter for someone to joke about how out of shape they are. The individuals who do not care about their physical health are merely showing to the world that they do not understand or do not care of the power and sophistication their own human body is capable of. If these individuals could only understand that they are walking around in something that would cost the government billions and billions of dollars to imperfectly replicate, then maybe they would take a little more time to think about the way they are treating their body.

Beginning a physical health improvement requires effort, and effort requires motivation. If you are ready to make a positive bodily change, you can start by understanding what it means to have proper motivation and how you can use your motivation to achieve your goals. You can then begin to understand the pros of positive physical health and the cons of negative physical health. When you fully understand the meaning and importance of proper motivation and the pros of positive physical health and the cons of negative physical health and feel you have gained enough energy to take direct action to making a positive change, you can begin to increase your chances of success by fully understanding what consist of proper physical health. When you have acquired enough knowledge and motivation to improve your physical health you can begin to learn, understand, and implement physical health solutions into your life such as, planning, determination, understanding intrinsic desire, understanding the importance of knowledge, taking it slow, making productive use of downtime and keeping a logbook. Following these guidelines will definitely increase your physical health. When you take the time to understand and respect your body, fully understanding what it means to live healthy you will never go back to the person you were before you started improving your physical health. The newly, vibrant, and refreshed individual you will become when you improve your physical health will allow you to understand more of the true meaning of total prosperity.

PROPER MOTIVATION

To take action and make a positive physical health change in your life requires you to have a certain amount of motivation. You have to become motivated enough to get off the couch and put down the potato chips and take action on the state of your physical well-being. Motivation to make a positive change is not something that can be store bought and it is not something that can be faked. Possessing the proper motivation to make a change is something that has to come from within. Proper motivation is a deep seeded driving force that enables you to fight off laziness, procrastination, and bad habits. The problem with someone who maintains negative physical health is not a lack of motivation, because we all have an ample supply of motivation in our bodies. You see living human beings are born with it. If you did not have motivation you would not be here to read this because without motivation, the sperm that was the beginnings of you would have never beat the other thousands of sperm to the egg, to create the person you are. The problem with many individuals is their motivation is a motivation based on negative and not positive. Over the years, individuals with negative motivations have slowly developed negative habits that have taken a comfortable residence in their mind. When a negative behavior becomes a comfortable resident in your mind, a negative motivation for that behavior has begun. Let me give you some examples, cigarette smoker's posses negative motivation. Their minds have motivated them to buy cigarettes and smoke cigarettes. Probably what happened for this negative motivation to occur in these individual's lives was that the cigarette was there for them at a particular time of need and the motivation to go back to that cigarette grew stronger. When someone first takes a puff of a cigarette, it is not pleasurable for him or her. It is the body's natural reaction to fight it by coughing, nausea, or headache. Many individuals begin this habit for several reasons; maybe it is peer pressure, boredom, or depression. The concern is not why these individuals started, but why they developed a negative motivation for cigarettes and when this negative motivation was allowed to become a comfortable resident in their mind. These individuals probably developed this negative motivation by allowing this motivation to give them pleasure. Maybe they found themselves feeling better if they had a cigarette after dinner or maybe they found themselves feeling relaxed if they had a cigarette after a stressful occurrence. The fact of the matter is, at some point in time they began to incorporate a negative habit in their life by allowing their mind to find comfort and pleasure in this negative motivation. It is important to understand that negative motivations can reside in many areas of your life. A negative motivation can be something that you do frequently that does not better yourself, waste your time, or actually decrease your mental and physical health. Some examples of negative motivations include: drinking too much alcohol and any other type of substance abuse, watching too much television, sleeping too much, having negative eating habits, and enjoying laziness. Negative motivations have a way of sneaking into your life and allowing you feel they are normal. There are individuals out there who even find the negative motivation of sleeping too much, as a natural part of their lives. These individuals probably found themselves depressed at some point in time and did not get out of bed when they should have. Maybe by sleeping in they felt they were hiding or avoiding all their problems, which in turn gave them a sense of peace and pleasure, leading to an occupancy in the mind, of an idea that over sleeping will give them a peace and comfort, eventually this idea takes up full residence in their mind resulting in a negative motivation where they find themselves sleeping at all hours of the day. Sleeping becomes a hobby for them. If it is a nice day and there are outside activities they could enjoy, their mind will tell them that they will get more enjoyment out of a nap on the couch than enjoying the pleasantries nature as to offer. In the process, these individuals grow unhealthier by the day creating a vicious negative cycle, making it harder and harder for these individuals to take direct action to improve themselves. The more you can understand of negative motivations, the more chance you will have at successfully turning your negative motivations into positive proper motivations. When you begin to realize that many of the things you do in life are nothing more than negative motivations and these negative motivations are the things holding you back from making positive actions to improving yourself, you will be able to revert these negative motivations and create new positive motivations.

For the sake of your health, it is important to realize that a physical health improvement cannot be accomplished without taking direct action. Having good intentions of wanting to change your physical health will not actually change your physical health. Action taken on those intentions is the only thing that will actually improve your physical health. Action takes energy, and the only way to get the proper energy is to have proper motivation in your life to make a physical health improvement. Proper motivations work in the same manner negative motivations do, the only difference between the two is proper motivations are motivations that improve yourself daily, increase your overall success rate, and increase your mental and physical health, and increase your life expectancy, and negative motivations do exactly the opposite. Proper motivations include: having healthy eating habits, using things in moderation such as drinking, exercising properly as much as possible, healthy and safe outdoor activities, and enjoying keeping your body in shape. Proper motivations are developed the same way negative motivations are. At some point in time the individuals who posses proper motivations found these motivations taking up a comfortable residence in their mind, giving them happiness and pleasure. Take someone who has the proper motivation of maintaining an exercising program for example. Just as with smoking, these individuals probably found their body is rejecting the exercise program at first due to it being difficult and strenuous, but at some point in time, these individuals found pleasure and solace in this activity, which in turn created a comfortable habitat in their mind and eventually caused a proper motivation in their life. Maybe one day they realized that when they exercised after work they felt a reduction in stress or maybe they realized they found themselves feeling more energetic after a workout and enjoyed the rush that exercising gave them. Either way, this proper motivation was able to find a comfortable residence in their mind, creating this positive motivation. When you begin to understand where and how your motivations are derived, you can begin to better understand how to achieve positive and proper motivations in your life.

The effects of the achievement of positive motivations in ones life are far reaching. When you begin to alleviate negative motivations from your life and substitute negative motivations with proper and positive motivations, you will begin to increase every aspect of your life. The understanding and realization of proper motivations will allow you the proper level of motivation and momentum to gather enough energy to take direct action on improving your physical health. You have to ask yourself, "do I want to have motivations that decrease my capabilities, happiness, success, physical and mental health, and life expectancy, or do I want motivations that are going to increase my capabilities, happiness, success, physical and mental health, and life expectancy?" I think the choice is clear. To become someone who is physically healthy and very prosperous, it is imperative that you destroy negative motivations in your life and begin to incorporate proper motivations into your life.

THE PROS & CONS OF PHYSICAL HEALTH

When you begin to develop positive proper motivation in your life, it is important to reinforce the proper motivation by understanding the pros of having positive physical health and the cons of having negative physical health. When you begin to understand the importance of your physical health and how many things in your life that good physical health can improve, you will begin to gain even more motivation to continue taking daily action on improving your physical health. There are times in our lives when we simply cannot find enough motivation to make a decision and make the change. There seems to be the question "should I", or "shouldn't I". Should I make the change or should I not make the change. When you become stuck on top of the fence, unable to make a decision and go in one particular direction is when you need to understand the pros and cons of that situation to allow you to move forward in the direction of the positives without any regret or frozen loss of action for the negatives. When you are able to see and understand the pros and cons of situations, it is much easier to take action and make a positive change in the direction of the pros instead of the cons. When you are unsure of the pros and cons of situations, it is much easier to stay frozen in the middle never taking action to make a change in the positive direction. Moreover, when you are standing still you are eventually going to be passed by and left behind. Physical health is no exception to the rule. If you want to make a positive change in your physical health, it is beneficial to know the pros and cons this decision will have on your life. When you begin to see the good things positive physical health can bring you and the unhealthy things negative physical health can bring you, it is much easier to stay motivated to take action on improving your physical health.

There are many positives to improving your physical health. One of the most important things of good physical health is that it can increase your life expectancy. Other important beneficial positives of good physical health include: an increase in energy, stamina, and vitality; a decrease in the risk of heart disease and cancer; an increase in confidence and self-worth; an increase in happiness and success; an increase in your bodies natural immune system; better sexual performance; an increase in muscle flexibility; an increased sense of self-fulfillment; an increase in recovery time from sickness and disease; a reduction in the ageing process; and an increase in proper motivations in your life. The list of positives for maintaining good physical health can go on and on. When you begin to realize all the positive things that can happen in your life when you improve your physical health, you will begin to understand why it is so important to maintain good physical health in your life. When there are so many positives in one solution such as good physical health, it should be no question that you should get off the couch and take action to improve you physical health.

The negatives or cons to maintaining unhealthy physical health are as vast as the positives are for maintaining good physical health. One major negative or con of negative physical health is a decrease in your life expectancy. It is a proven fact that if you maintain negative and unhealthy physical health you will be shortening your life! That con alone should be reason enough to gain the proper motivation to make an improvement in your physical health. Other negatives to unhealthy physical health include: a decrease in your energy and stamina; an increase of fatigue; an increased risk of heart disease and cancers; an increased risk of obesity; a decrease in confidence and self-esteem; an increased risk of depression and anxiety; lowered sexual stamina and performance; an increased chance of injury in the form of pulled and strained muscles and back injuries; and an increase in developed negative motivations in your life. When it becomes clear that there are just as many, if not more cons of negative physical health as pros of good physical health, the decision should become clear as to which direction you need to be headed in.

To gain proper motivation to allow yourself the energy to take action on improving your physical health, it is time to understand the positives of good physical health and the negatives of poor physical health. When you begin see the pros and cons of good and poor physical health, it is clear to see which one is more beneficial to your life and which will improve the quality of your life. When you reach the point where you clearly see which the wisest decision to make and which decision will bring you the most health and happiness is the point you need to take action and improve your physical health.

WHAT CONSIST OF PROPER PHYSICAL HEALTH

When you have gained the proper motivation to take action on improving your physical health, it is important that you understand all that consist of physical health. To become someone who possesses well-rounded good physical health you need to improve every aspect of your physical health, which includes strength training, cardiovascular training, and flexibility training. When you can improve on all three facets of physical health equally, you will become an individual who possess a full form of good physical health. It is important that you give equal time to improving all three because making an improvement on one does not qualify as well-rounded good physical health. There are individuals who do nothing but weight train and have no cardiovascular health and there are individuals who do nothing but cardiovascular training but lack in physical muscular strength due to lack of training. To become fully physically fit it is crucial you understand what consist of well-rounded physical health and you improve on all facets of physical health.

Strength training is one facet of physical health. When you begin your physical health improvement, you should incorporate strength-training exercises as part of your program. Strength training involves the part of your physical health where you tone and strengthen your bodily muscles. When strength training is accomplished successfully it will strength and improve your bodies muscle functions, creating a better, more fit physical body. When you create stronger muscles, your body becomes less prone to physical injury and more prone to fight off illnesses. Proper strength training involves resistance training with things such as, free weights or nautilus equipment. When you train with resistance, you are forcing particular muscles to work and break themselves down alone to repair themselves stronger. It is important to understand that strength training is part of well-rounded physical health and it must be incorporated in your improvement phase if you want to possess total physical health.

Cardiovascular training is another aspect of well-rounded physical health. Cardiovascular training and improvement is the part of physical health that can help decrease heart disease and increase energy and stamina. Some examples of cardiovascular training include: running, walking, swimming, and biking. Cardiovascular exercises are the exercises that are going to cause you to increase your heart rate and break a sweat. Proper cardiovascular training can do many positive things such as increase your life's health potentials and fight off obesity by burning off unwanted calories. To obtain well-rounded good physical health it is important to spend as much time on your cardiovascular improvement as you do your strength training improvement. For without cardiovascular and strength training working together as a team to improve the body and fight off the negatives, they will merely be working alone and out numbered. If you incorporate both of these facets of physical health together, you will be able to improve on a much greater level than merely making an improvement on just one.

Flexibility training is an important aspect of physical health that is often overlooked. Much of the soreness and injuries that people experience are associated with poor flexibility. Flexibility training involves the part of your physical health that increases your muscle limberness. For example, your muscles can be equated to rubber bands, the more your flexibility increases and improves, the more you will be able to stretch those rubber bands, being your muscles, and have them fall back into place without them tearing, ripping, or straining. When you try to stretch an old rubber band that has lost its elasticity it usually tears or breaks immediately, but when you stretch a new fresh rubber band, it can stretch out to extreme links without sometimes every breaking. The same can be thought of with you muscles. When your body is performing a physical activity such as running or jumping the muscles are constantly being stretched like a rubber band. How much they can stretch will depend on the level of performance, soreness and injury you may experience from this physical activity. The more your muscles can stretch the better they will perform and the less likely they are to rupture, sprain, tear, and pull. The more stiffness and tightness your muscles possess the more likely they are to cause a decrease in performance and an increase in injury. Therefore, if you want total well-rounded physical health where you can perform to your full potential you should incorporate flexibility training in your physical health improvements.

Before you begin your physical health improvement, it is important you understand all that consist of physical health. When you fully understand that well-rounded physical health consist of strength training, cardiovascular training, and flexibility training, you will be ready to begin a successful physical health improvement. When you realize what fully consist of well-rounded physical health, you will be able to understand that you cannot possess total physical health without improving all facets of physical health, which are strength fitness, cardiovascular fitness, and flexibility fitness. You will begin to understand that if you do not improve all three facets of good physical health together as a team, you will not be able to experience and maximize the positives good physical health can bring you. When strength, cardiovascular, and flexibility training are incorporated in your physical health improvement, you will be able to utilize and experience all the positives that good physical health can offer. You will then begin to see what it feels like to possess well-rounded good physical health.

SOLUTIONS TO IMPROVING YOUR PHYSICAL HEATLH

When you begin to understand how proper motivation can give you the energy to take action and improve and what consist of physical health, you can begin the process of improving your physical health. On your journey of physical health improvement, many helpful solutions can aid you along the way. These helpful solutions are designed to make your physical health improvement easier and more successful. When you incorporate these solutions into your life you will be on a proven track for results and success. The solutions that will aid you along the way to physical health improvement include: planning, determination, understanding intrinsic desire, understanding the importance of knowledge, taking it slow, making productive use of downtime and keeping a log. When you implement these helpful solutions into your physical health improvement phase, you will be able to achieve a much greater rate of success.

Planning is an important part of a successful physical health improvement. Without a proper plan of attack, it will be very difficult to make a successful improvement. When you begin your physical health improvement, you should first draw up a well-organized plan of attack. Realize what you are trying to accomplish and set your plan accordingly. If you are overweight and desire to lose unwanted body fat, you should set a plan that puts emphasis on heavy cardiovascular and light strength training and flexibility training until you have reached your desired weight loss. At the point you have achieved your desired goal, you can then revise the plan to have a well balance between the three. If you feel you are lacking in muscle definition and strength but are not overweight, you may want to set a plan to begin heavy on strength training and flexibility and light on cardiovascular training. When you have achieved your desired muscle definition, you can revise the plan to balance out the three. Your physical health plan should be a personal plan that is precise and descriptive to your desired needs. Make a daily and weekly plan for what type of improvements you want to make. A simple beginning plan can look something like this, Monday, Wednesday, and Friday strength and flexibility training and Tuesday and Thursday cardiovascular training, for thirty minutes per day. A plan like this will help you determine what you are going to work on and for how long. When you get a little more advanced you can begin to break down the plan in more detail such as, what type of cardiovascular training and what muscle groups you intend to work on. A well-organized plan is the first helpful solution to incorporate if you desire to achieve a successful physical health improvement.

Learning the importance of determination can be a very helpful solution to improving your physical health. Determination is the feeling people get that allows them to accomplish something successfully no matter who or what gets in the way. Someone who is determined to improve their physical health will put all their priority on accomplishing this improvement. They will find themselves training even when they do not feel like it because they are filled with determination. An individual who is not fully determined will let their daily feelings affect their goal achievement. Someone who is not fully determined to improve their physical health will only train when they feel like training. If they are tired or simply do not feel like training on a particular day they will avoid and put off their training regime in order to meet their daily feelings because it is simply not that important to them. If you want to achieve total success at your physical health improvement, it is imperative that you make yourself become fully determined to achieve this goal. Realize the importance this physical health improvement will have on your health, happiness, and success and make it a determination in your life to improve your physical health successfully. Becoming filled with determination will allow you to put aside and ignore your daily vicissitudes. This will allow you to stay completely focused, consistent, and persistent to the goal of improving your physical health.

Understanding the importance of intrinsic desire is a helpful solution that can increase your overall determination for the success of your physical health improvement. Intrinsic desire is something that comes totally from within. It is a deep driving force that you feel inside. People who are intrinsically motivated for self-improvement are proven to have a much greater success rate over those who are extrinsically motivated. An individual who is intrinsically motivated is someone who is deeply motivated to do something for their own self, regardless of what others think and feel. An individual who is extrinsically motivated is someone who does something for others and the motivation is based solely on what others think and feel. Let us use physical health improvement for an example. An individual who is intrinsically motivated to make a physical health improvement is motivated to make this improvement on their own with no outside intervention, their desire to train and improve their physical health daily is based on things such as, their pure inner desire to want to better themselves, the personal fulfillment they receive when they are training, and the personal enjoyment they feel when they are training. An individual who is extrinsically motivated to make a physical health improvement is motivated to make this improvement by outside forces, their desire to train and improve their physical health daily is based on things such as, their spouse saying they want them to look better, a friend saying they have seen someone in a magazine that they thought was attractive, so now this extrinsic motivated individual wants to look like that, there is nothing on television, or the poker game was canceled, the list of extrinsic reasons to train and improve can go on and on and until you can change your desires for improvement from extrinsic to intrinsic you will never be able to achieve full success. The reason is, extrinsic desire or motivation is fleeting and inconsistent, it is moment to moment depending on what others are wanting or what other occurrences in your life are or are not happening that allow you to train and improve or not to train and improve, and intrinsic desire or motivation is steady like a rock and consistent, it is internal desire to improve no matter who is saying other wise or what the situation is, it is simply a pure desire to improve based on driven intrinsic motivation coming from within. When you begin your physical health improvement, it is important you base your improvements on your own intrinsic desires, not the desire of others or the convenience of situations. When you become intrinsically motivated and determined to improve your physical health, you will make it a reality of your own and it will happen successfully.

When you begin your physical health improvement, it is important that you read and study all you can about physical health and nutrition. In any situation in life, the more knowledge and education you have, the better off you will be. Physical health is no exception. The more knowledge you have of things that pertain to good physical such as, how the body works, the proper steps to take when improving the body, what to eat, when and how much to sleep, when to exercise, how to properly exercise, and what body groups to exercise, the more your chances will be of making a successful physical health improvement. There is nothing worse than an individual exhausting all their means to improving their physical health improperly, due to a lack of knowledge. Trying to make a blind, futile, uneducated attempt at improving your physical health is unhealthy, discouraging, dangerous, and nothing more than a waste of time. If you feel you are very naive and lack in knowledge on the subject of improving your physical health then you should begin to study the subject as much as possible before you attempt to make the improvement. It is impossible to have too much knowledge on the subject of physical health and quite frankly, the more knowledge you have of physical health, the more successful your improvements will become. You can gain the proper knowledge of physical health in many areas; it does not have to be limited to books and magazines. You can visit a nutritionist, find a professional trainer, or see a local physician for advice and knowledge on physical health and the proper way to make a physical health improvement. If you desire to make a successful physical health improvement the amount of knowledge you have on the subject of physical health will be a determining factor on the amount of success you achieve on your personal physical health improvements.

Gaining the patience to take it slow is a solution that will help you avoid discouragement and injury. When you begin your physical health improvement, you should take baby steps to achieve the final goal successfully. It is important to understand that excellent physical condition does not come overnight and it will require a great deal of time and patience to achieve a total physical health improvement. To achieve successful improvement on your physical health, begin as slow and as light as you can until you have developed enough energy and confidence to increase the pace. If you jump right into a physical health improvement wide open you are more than likely going to get discouraged, burned out, or injured, either of which cause eventual quitting or long periods of stopping. By taking it slow and light you will allow your body and mind to become adjusted and familiarized with the physical change it is experiencing.

Another helpful solution to successful physical health improvement is to make productive use of your downtime. You see, many times throughout the day we experience absolute downtime. Downtime in a sense that there is nothing to do immediately and you have full choice of what you want to do. Downtime can be anywhere at anytime, some examples of downtime include: the time you have in the mornings before you leave work after you have eaten breakfast, the time just before lunch or just after lunch, a job break, when you are waiting in line or when you are stuck at traffic lights or stuck in traffic, vacations, and weekends. A popular downtime for many individuals in America is the time just after work and just before dinner. Another popular downtime for Americans is the time just after dinner and just before bed, usually about seven pm to nine thirty pm. The television networks like to refer to this particular downtime as "primetime" and there is a perfectly good reason for that. This particular downtime is a large percentage of most individual's daily downtime and the majority of average people enjoy using this particular downtime perched in front of a television set where they are able to use just a slight bit more brain power than they would if they were sleeping. That is right; it is a proven scientific fact that when human beings are watching television they are using only a slight more percentage of brainpower than when they are sleeping. In a sense, when you are watching television you are in a vegetative state. With this in mind, the majority of individuals who go into a vegetative state at "primetime" generally enjoy similar vegetative states at all courses of their daily downtime. If you are wanting to make a physical health improvement or overall improvement for that matter, it is important that you become aware of your downtime and begin to make your downtime more productive. If you find yourself watching television every night and fighting to find the time to exercise, then you should wean yourself off the televising habits and find time to exercise during "primetime", and believe me it will make you feel better than turning yourself into a vegetable for two hours. Therefore, if you want to improve your physical health put a head of lettuce in front of the television to take your place and find the time to make a physical health improvement. Using the smaller downtime during the day can be an excellent time to work on your physical improvement plan or focus on you physical improvement goals. If you are stuck in traffic or stuck waiting on an appointment, instead of drifting off or worrying about stuff you have no control over, take the time to focus on the things you want to improve on and accomplish or read something that is going to improve your knowledge on the subject of your improvement. Making productive use of your downtime will allow you to better achieve success at your physical health improvement and allow you to get the most potential out of your life.

Keeping a log of your improvements is a helpful way to let allow you to track your progress. When you are in the process of improving your physical health, you should keep a logbook of your daily progress. During your strength training, you can keep a log of how much weight you are lifting and what exercises you are using. In your cardiovascular training, you can keep a log of the duration, time, and heart rate of your training and you can log how you felt after each training regimen. In your flexibility training, you can log how far you are able to stretch each muscle and the duration you are able to hold that stretch. At the end of the month, this log will prove vital; because it will allow you to clearly see your improvements and see what areas, you need improving on. It is important to keep a logbook of all of your life's improvement phases, so you can clearly see the progress you are making or the lack of progress you are making. When you can clearly see it on paper you will be able to attack the areas you are lacking in and succeed.

CONCLUSION

Physical health is an important aspect of total prosperity. If you do not posses good physical health or do not desire to possess good physical health, you will never allow your body to reach its full potential and you will never be able to experience all the positives that good physical health can bring to your life. If you are on the quest to total prosperity, it is important you understand and realize the importance good physical can have in your life and it is important to realize that total prosperity can never be obtained without incorporating good physical health in your life. To make a physical health improvement in your life, you will need to understand what it means to have proper motivation and how you can use proper motivation to gain energy to take action and achieve your goals. You should fully understand the pros of good physical health and the cons of poor physical health to fully motivate you into making a successful physical health improvement. When you have fully understood the meaning and importance of proper motivation and the positives of good physical health and the negatives of poor physical health, you should begin to increase your knowledge of physical health improvement by fully understanding that well-rounded physical health consist of strength training, cardiovascular training, and flexibility training.

174

When you have fully understood the meaning of proper motivation, the positives of good physical health, the negatives of poor physical health, and what consist of a well-rounded good physical health, you can begin to implement helpful physical health solutions into your life such as, planning, determination, understanding intrinsic desire, understanding the importance of knowledge, taking it slow, making productive use of downtime, and keeping a logbook, to help you successfully achieve your desired physical health improvement. When you take action and become determined to improving your physical health, not only will you be improving your physical body, you will be improving every aspect of your life as well, drawing you closer to a life filled with total prosperity.

Speed bumps are on every road that leads to prosperity!!!!!

CONCLUDING

THE SEVEN STEPS TO TOTAL prosperity include Time Management, Stress management, Spiritual Health, Frame of Mind, Relationships, Eating Habits, and Physical Health. When you begin to understand and master these seven steps you will find yourself living in total prosperity. You life will become mentally, physically, spiritually, and financially successful. Living in total prosperity, will bring you the most enjoyment, happiness, and success that life has to offer. You will put your old Average self behind you and become a new, refreshed individual with a newfound positive respect for life and all the happiness it can bring. Living in total prosperity will allow you to realize that you cannot live in total happiness by merely being prosperous in one area of your life. You will realize that to acquire true-life happiness you will need to become prosperous in all areas of prosperity, which include being prosperous financially, spiritually, mentally, and physically. You will also have the means of obtaining totally prosperity in all these areas by understanding and following the seven steps or pathways to total prosperity. You will understand that each step to prosperity must be used in a balanced form, working together as a team to achieve your goal of living a life full of happiness and success possessing total prosperity.

If you are ready to achieve total prosperity in your life, it is time to make a positive change in your life and become fully determined to follow the seven steps to total prosperity. You can do this by mastering your time management skills to get make the most productivity out of the time you have, by mastering your stress management skills to allow yourself to better control your life's daily hardships, by increasing your spiritual health to allow more peace and happiness into your life, by creating a more positive frame of mind to improve your daily perception of life, by improving your relationships to create more happiness, success, and positive opportunities in your life, by incorporating good eating habits to improve your mental and physical well-being, and by improving your physical health to increase your happiness, energy, vitality, and life expectancy. When you follow these seven steps to total prosperity in a determined and urgent manner, experiencing total prosperity in your life will become inevitable. The seven steps to total prosperity are designed to increase your health and happiness internally and externally, which will allow you to separate yourself from the average, by being emotionally, financially, spiritually, mentally, and physically prosperous and successful, and that is the true definition of TOTAL PROSPERITY. Please allow yourself the opportunity to experience an elated life of total prosperity by passionately following the seven steps to total prosperity everyday of your life.

Happiness & Success in life is yours for the taking!!

REPORT CARD

      I HAVE ENCLOSED A DAILY report card in the back of this book. It is designed to let you know exactly how each day of your life is progressing while you are trying to achieve total prosperity, it is also designed to have the positive words in this book be with you everyday, instead of getting temporarily inspired after reading only to lose the inspiration by mid-afternoon because you have forgotten the positive words you read. By grading yourself on your daily performance, you will never be able to leave the book being and forget about the inspiring words. To score highly on the report card, you will need to constantly focus on the seven steps to total prosperity until you have completely mastered all of them. This allows you to never forget about the book and the positive words it has to offer. You can make copies of the original to track your daily progress and improvements. At the end of each day, take a moment to yourself and look back on the day. While you are looking back on the days events, give yourself grades on how you feel your were in each of the seven steps of total prosperity. See how well your time management skills, stress management skills, spiritual health, frame of mind, relationships, eating habits, and physical health stood up to the test and hardships of real daily life. Give yourself a grade between 0 and 15 in each of the seven steps; zero being the lowest or poorest grade and fifteen being the highest or best grade. This grading is very important because it will be directly linked to your daily happiness and prosperity and you will be able to clearly see on paper, what went wrong and where. Your daily scores will begin to tell you exactly the type of happiness and prosperity you experienced. For example, if you were to live a day in total prosperity your score would be a perfect 105 percent. If you were to live a day in Average land, your score would be around 50 percent. This report card will also allow you to see exactly where you need the most improving. You may find yourself scoring highly in some areas and scoring low in others. The steps of prosperity where the scores are low will be the steps that will require the most effort and concentration to improve. I recommend that you grade yourself as strict as you can, allowing no slack in any of the seven steps. This grade is not one you are going to show someone to receive positive recognition. This is a personal grade that no one needs to see but you; it is designed to track your daily improvements and shortcomings to help you successfully achieve total prosperity with success. The stricter your grading can be, the better you will develop in each of the seven steps of total prosperity. Remember by giving yourself false high marks on your daily report cards, you will only be cheating yourself. Your goal should be to thrive for 105 percent on the report card everyday because that is where you will find total prosperity. The higher your daily score, the closer you will be to achieving total prosperity. If scored honestly, your daily scores may be a little low at first or they may fluctuate from high to low, but the more you begin to develop and master each step of total prosperity, your scores will begin to get consistently higher. When you are consistently achieving daily scores of 100 percent and over, regardless of the daily circumstances, then I have but this to say, "CONGRADULATONS & WELCOME TO THE WORLD OF TOTAL PROSPERITY!!!!!!!"

Daily Report Card

CATEGORY	TOTAL SCORE	PERSONAL SCORE
TIME MANAGEMENT	15	
STRESS MANAGEMENT	15	
SPIRITUAL HEALTH	15	
FRAME OF MIND	15	
RELATIONSHIPS	15	
DIET	15	
PHYSICAL HEALTH	15	

	MAXIMUM TOTAL	PERSONAL TOTAL
TOTAL DAILY SCORE	**105%**	

GRADING SCALE		
90-105 = A	*"Total*	*Prosperity"*
80-89 = B		
70-79 = C		
60-69 = D		
50-59 = F		

ABOUT THE AUTHOR

Rhett Smith is 28 years old and resides in Atlanta, Georgia with his wife Sherry Smith. He attended Kennesaw State University and is a successful entrepreneur of two companies and growing. How to continually overcome life's adversity and succeed with total prosperity is something Rhett has been able to accomplish. The knowledge of how he is able to accomplish this is what he wants to deliver to the reader. The ability to help people live a positive, healthy, happy, successful, soulful, and prosperous life is a passion of his.

Printed in the United States
1182500007B/115-132